S

D0396625

THE MASTIFF AND BULLMASTIFF
HANDBOOK

THE MASTIFF
AND BULLMASTIFF
HANDBOOK

Douglas B. Oliff

THE BOYDELL PRESS · HOWELL BOOK HOUSE

S

© D. B. Oliff 1988

First published 1988
by The Boydell Press
an imprint of Boydell & Brewer Ltd
PO Box 9, Woodbridge, Suffolk IP12 3DF
and by Howell Book House
Macmillan Publishing Company
866 Third Avenue, New York, NY 10022

Reprinted 1988, 1989, 1991

ISBN 0 85115 485 9

British Library Cataloguing in Publication Data
Oliff, D. B.
The mastiff and bullmastiff handbook.
1. Mastiff – History 2. Bullmastiff – History
I. Title
636.7'3'09   SF429.M36
ISBN 0 85115 485 9

Library of Congress Cataloging-in-Publication Data applied for

Printed in the United States of America

Dedication

This book is dedicated to my dogs both past, and present. It is recognition not only of their companionship and devotion, but the opportunity afforded of studying, and, I hope, understanding this unique canine group.

D. B. Oliff
June 1987

Errata and Addenda

Page 5   Third paragraph. De Foix wrote his treatise in French, and it was of course only 'published' in a few manuscript copies. Evidence now suggests that not Edmund de Langley, but Edward 2nd Duke of York translated a copy of the manuscript whilst he was imprisoned in Pevensey Castle from 1406 to 1413. He omitted some of the de Foix chapters, added chapters of his own then presented it as an original work as *The Master of Game*.

Page 18   Caption beneath the illustration to read: Illustration of mastiff and bulldog in the style of Bewick, published 1816.

Page 31   First sentence of last paragraph to read: King's granddam (not 'dam' as printed).
Appendix referred to in sixth paragraph of p. 31, omitted from the first printing, now inserted on the last page of the book.

Page 53   Bottom caption to read: Brockwell of *Goring*.

Page 67   Line 2 to read Ch. *Hotspot* of Havengore.

Page 88   Illustrations to be numbered:

2		3
	1	
4		5

Page 89   Second paragraph to read: The ribs are connected to the thirteen dorsal vertebrae the seven lumbar vertebrae are not supported by the ribs.

Page 115   To read: *See* pedigrees . . . (not, as printed, 'Sire pedigrees . . .').

Page 148   Illustrations to be numbered:

2		3
	1	
4		5

Page 154   First line under caption: Ch: *Craigylea* Sir Galahad; last line Ch: *Pitmans* Gentleman Jim.

Page 191   Second paragraph, sixth line to read: Switzerland.

Page 193   Caption to read: One of Germany's leading mastiff bitches.

Contents

Acknowledgements

My grateful thanks go to all those who have made this publication possible.

I appreciate the kindness of those who have taken the trouble to send me photographs of their dogs. What is particularly appreciated is the co-operation given by Mrs A. Davies of Tregaron who loaned many old photographs from her considerable collection. Owners the world over are interested in the history of the breeds, hence the comprehensive photographic collection many of which have never been previously published.

Miss M. E. Perrenoud kindly supplied a photograph of her first mastiff, and credit must go to Mrs S. Monostori whose landscape photograph with her Ch: Balint of Havengore in the foreground adorns the dust cover.

The line drawings by Graham Hurst considerably elucidate points made in the text and as such are invaluable to any breed publication.

My final thanks are to the publishers who have been tolerant and supportive during the production of the book.

D. B. Oliff
Woolaston, Lydney, Glos.

Foreword

Juliette de Bairacli Levy

A book on the Mastiff and Bullmastiff is an event in the world of animal books. With Douglas Oliff as the author it will make its mark for sure, and will be something not only to read, but to remember. Douglas Oliff is not only an expert on the subject of mastiffs of all kinds, he is a lifetime, and deep lover of these dogs. He is the appointed correspondent on Mastiffs for the English *Dog World*, and people from all over the world seek his advice on their history, and the successful rearing of these breeds. His Wyaston prefix was well known in bullmastiffs, and many great dogs carry the prefix in their pedigrees.

He is a great admirer of rural England, and deprecates unnatural farming practices especially the use of artificial fertilisers, toxic sprays and denatured food. He has followed my method of natural rearing for many generations and not only his dogs, but his very well known strain of Old English Game give evidence of the stamina which his feeding and rearing methods produce.

I have known the author for very many years and admire mastiffs because of what he has taught me about them in his interesting letters and our meetings at dog shows. His family was well known to me during the war when I worked in his beloved Forest of Dean, Gloucestershire, and it was in his home county that I acquired much gipsy lore of herbal treatments of animal ailments.

As a young child I met the mastiff when it was one of the breeds of rural England. My father was a collector of English and French antiquities and at weekends would drive us in his pony and trap (using his horse which he had brought with him from Turkey) to visit old mansions of the Lancashire and Cheshire areas. There I saw the mastiffs. Not only were they guardians of the great houses, but accompanied the gamekeepers who needed the protection of such a valiant breed when poachers of game were often armed, and dangerous.

Dr Johnson spoke of the courage of the mastiff and is quoted in that nostalgic book *The Ladies of Llangollen*.

My old Shropshire Nanny, Alice Emily Sedgely used to encourage us children to be 'brave as a mastiff'.

I am pleased to write this foreword to what will be a classic for many years to come and a reference book for all interested in these historic and great breeds of dog.

Preface

Within the mind of every dog owner, there appears to be an ardent desire to prove the antiquity of his chosen breed. Whenever one picks up a specific breed handbook, it is normal for the author to devote the first chapter to the breed's history, usually by stating that the breed is one whose roots are found in the earliest times. The only exceptions are those breeds of more recent evolution, but even these are often claimed to have been based on breeds of great antiquity.

So much of this so-called 'history' is misconception and supposition. There are references to dogs from the earliest periods of civilisation onwards, but such references are loosely applied by most writers of breed history. The resulting accounts and descriptions are of doubtful accuracy, so there comes a time when a reappraisal of historical facts becomes necessary.

In outlining the history of the mastiff, I have made an effort to publish only those facts which can be substantiated as being reasonably accurate. There are few breeds which have been subjected to as much irrational, and unfounded historical balderdash as the mastiff. Much is due to the unashamed piracy of canine journalists throughout the ages. When an original mistake becomes repeated by subsequent writers, it is eventually accepted as fact.

Critics will probably accuse me of unnecessary iconoclasm when statements which have been accepted as being factual for generations are held up to closer scrutiny, and disproved. If the history of the breed is to be written, it must be factual, even if, by stripping away some of the fables of time, we disturb a few unsound superstructures.

This is the first occasion on which there has been an attempt to combine in one book the various aspects of two breeds which show such close consanguinity, and to demonstrate that throughout the recorded history of the mastiff, mastiffs which carried the bulldog cross have contributed to its evolution.

1

Early Mastiff History

The breed has been blessed with one great historian and scholar, a Victorian clergyman, Rev. M. B. Wynn, who published his exhaustive 'History of the Mastiff' in 1886. The extent of his research for this work was amazing, and his abilities to collect data phenomenal. It is a classic, but a Victorian classic in which imagination plays no small part. Speaking geometrically, Wynn, who was a brilliant Latin scholar, worked his *quod erat demonstrandum* first, then worked his theorem back from there. By and large he assembled facts which proved his theories, but dismissed as ill-informed opinion anything which suggested that his theories were wrong. There are aspects of the book with which I cannot agree, but this does not mean that I do not appreciate his work. I consider that this very rare publication should be studied by any serious student of the breed, and even though one cannot agree with the history as recorded by Wynn, his assessment of mastiff type is masterly.

Wynn was convinced that the mastiff, as it appeared to him in the late nineteenth century, was the animal found in Britain from the earliest times. He was also convinced that a dog with a truncated muzzle, and broad mouth, of the type accepted as the true mastiff in his time, was the same as the fundamental type. He conceded that the ancient dog was not as large as the mastiff of his day, and therefore found it necessary to import some other breed to greatly increase the size of the indigenous type. His basic theory in chapter 2 of his book comes nearer to the truth when he writes: 'The theory or opinion that I hold is that the English mastiff from the earliest times has existed in Britain, in its purity resembling in many ways a vast bulldog, being ancestor of that breed. Such being the true *pugnaces* peculiar to Britain and Gaul mentioned by the historians, and by crossing these larger breeds, particularly the Asiatic mastiff (introduced probably by the Phoenicians) and other large races of *pugnaces*, such as the white Alan, a larger variety of mastiff was formed'.

My theory is quite different. I agree that the rudimentary mastiff type was indigenous to Britain, but it was not as large as, or in any way very similar to today's conception of the breed. There were considerable variations in size, but any large dog of guarding ability was frequently called a 'mastiff', the word being used to describe a variety of animals rather than a specific breed. The mastiff as we know it today is the product of mid-nineteenth century breeding, which will be proved later in the book.

What puzzled Wynn was how to adequately account for the greatly increased size in the modern mastiff, after admitting that the British *pugnax* was not a large dog. Ovid's contemporary, Gratius Faliscus, writing about AD 6 records that the British *pugnaces* were pitted against the *pugnaces* of Epirus, and beat them. Strabo in AD 44 remarks on the Celtic use of 'war dogs of pendant ears, lowering aspect, and flabby lips'. Wynn was aware of these writings so evolved the theory that Asiatic mastiffs were used to give the necessary size. He quoted the lion hunting dogs as depicted on the bas reliefs in the British Museum taken from the Temple of Konyunjik, showing the Assyrian King Assurbanipal engaged in his favourite hunting sport, as being the 'imports' used as a cross on our native breed.

This to me is a question of the author's assumption of quite unproven facts, moulded to prove his theory. Wynn must have known that it was highly improbable that any dog as large as the mastiff of his day was in Britain in those primitive times, or for many centuries afterwards, but Assurbanipal's hounds appeared a likely answer to his problem. With some skill, and far greater imagination the importation of the Asiatic mastiffs was attributed to the Phoenicians, a theory still being repeated today. If nothing else, Wynn set the pattern for the many who have blindly followed a theory which does not bear scrutiny.

The Phoenician Theory

There is no evidence of Phoenician contacts with Britain. The supposition that they were traders in Cornish tin arose from an account of a Phoenician named Himilco who thought that his journey took him to Cornwall. As this account attributed to Himilco was penned some 800 years after his death by Avenius, its authenticity is very questionable. Dr Harden, a world authority on the Phoenicians with whom I have discussed the theory, states that there is no evidence whatsoever to suggest that Phoenicians ever reached Britain. In his opinion, Assurbanipal's hunting dogs are exactly the same as dogs on Roman mosaics of some 1,000 years later. Dr Harden reminded me that many artists learnt from pattern books, and designs were not only similar in many countries, but were used over a long period of time. The dogs on the Assyrian bas-reliefs may look alike, but this cannot be translated as being proof that they were one identical breed, as the artist probably used the same outline throughout. If one studies the features of the dog handlers in the bas reliefs, these too are almost identical.

To look logically at the Phoenician theory, is it likely that these astute traders would bring something as unwieldy and perishable as a live mastiff, as an article of barter? The sea-going Phoenicians travelled in ships which consisted of two banks of oars and a deck above. Conditions in such vessels were extremely cramped for the crew, and their cargo. Even with today's refinements of canned diet, I would not consider the chances of a mastiff surviving the journey on such a ship, and under similar conditions, to be very great. It would need a Thor Heyerdahl to provide the theory, and undertake the journey, but who would subject a dog to the conditions of such primitive travel?

R. D. Bennett, Head of the Department of Western Asiatic Studies at the British Museum with whom the theory was discussed, states in a letter to me

'. . . there is no evidence whatsoever to suppose that dogs were ever brought by the Phoenicians'.

We can safely dismiss the Phoenician theory, and attempt to visualise Britain's *pugnax* as found by the Romans.

The Roman Era

The Roman writer Faliscus mentioned earlier in this chapter wrote his *Cynegeticon Liber* as verses describing the pleasures of the hunt and the qualities of the hounds. Among his listed imports is the 'Briton'. This was a fighting breed as Faliscus considered it 'almost worthwhile making the journey to those far shores to obtain one of this breed, as the courage and ferocity is unmatched by any other breed'. This seems convincing evidence of a unique fighting dog existing in Britain, and that they found their way to Rome. Unlike the sea-faring Phoenicians of a much earlier period, one must remember that Roman Legions travelled through Europe on foot, and that transporting dogs was therefore a possibility. One theory which Wynn disposed of was the hoary tale of the Romans appointing a Procurator for the purpose of watching over the interests of dogs, and exporting them to Rome. Camden was the originator of the mistake by confusing the Latin words *cynoecii* and *cynegii*. There was a *Procurator Cynoecii* responsible for the weaving of fine cloths and their subsequent export to Rome, but he was in no way connected with dogs.

The primitive Britons took dogs into battle against the invading Roman. From this fact emerged the fable of the mastiffs accompanying Queen Boadicea in her chariots and fighting with her in her rebellion against the Romans.

Again we must analyse the facts and prove the inaccuracy of the story. The very name is erroneous. The lady in question was Queen Boudicca and the stories of her scythe-mouthed chariot wheels are pure fiction. Perhaps the mastiff and Boudicca theory has been encouraged by Thorneycroft's statue which stands on the London Embankment. Here Boudicca rides in equestrian splendour in what always appears to me to be an armoured milk float. A true replica of a British war chariot of this era can be found in the National Museum of Wales. The total floor space of the vehicle is approximately three feet square. One can imagine the contortions necessary for the full bodied Boudicca to ride, accompanied by her monstrous *pugnax*. Colourful though the story may be, Boudicca's mastiffs can be dismissed as safely as her lethal chariot wheels, although one cannot but admire this valiant, if somewhat bloodthirsty, Celtic Queen.

Before closing our brief look at the mastiff of Roman times, perhaps we should consider the name *molossus*, as in some ancient writings the two words, *molossus* and mastiff, are considered to be synonymous. The *molossus* was a large dog which is said to have originated from Epirus, on the Greek mainland opposite the island of Corfu. It was, apparently, a crop-eared, square-headed dog with a heavy mane giving it a leonine appearance, named after Molossus, the king of Epirus, who invaded and waged war on southern Italy. This mastiff-type dog was used as a cross on native Roman breeds, and while there was undoubtedly a similarity of temperament between it, and the British *pugnax*, it is unlikely that there was close blood relationship between the two. Like the Roman dog, the British dog was farm dog, hound, or watchdog, according to its size or type.

In my opinion the whole history of the mastiff would be made far easier if it is accepted that the mastiff of the many historical quotations signifies a family type, and not a specific breed, and only remotely resembling the breed in its present form. I find it difficult to understand how a person of Wynn's intelligence could not have realised that dogs of the mastiff type were distributed throughout the world, each specific to its environment. It is pointless in speculating that at this stage any of the family helped to evolve the other. When we consider that the wolf was distributed throughout the northern hemisphere, we do not need a Phoenician to transport a stud wolf from Siberia to ancient Britain. Animals such as the horse and ass are found universally and one appreciates that in recent times the Arab horse has been used on native stock, but would a Tibetan pony have to trace its ancestry to our New Forest or Dartmoor types? There were large dogs in Central Asia during and long before the Roman civilisation, and it seems to me that Assurbanipal's hunting dogs were probably similar to the present day Anatolian Karabash. Geographically this is possible.

During the Han Dynasty of China (206 BC – 220 AD) there were several sculptures of short haired dogs of the mastiff type, with broad truncated muzzles. Judging by the strength of the harness which these models were wearing, they were obviously powerful dogs, with broad chests and short, strong legs.

Much speculation, and very few authenticated definitions have been given to the word 'alan' or 'alaunt', names which in earlier times were used to describe what appears to have been a mastiff type. Wynn considered the name to have been derived from the fierce Alani tribes, natives of the Caucasus who swept through Europe prior to the Roman colonisation. The fact that such brief accounts as are available state that the alans were white was sufficient to suggest to Wynn that his theory was correct, and that the animals were 'probably Russian in origin'. Wynn, who never lacked imagination, considered that the Siberian Mastiffs were white, yet records that when he owned a 'Russian Mastiff' it was deep chestnut red, with blue or slate-coloured points. Not content with this contradiction, he wrote that he considered this to be a true mastiff colour as he had once seen an English Mastiff of similar colour which was the property of Lord Stanley. Even by Wynn's standards, this was a sweeping statement, generalising on the colour as the result of seeing two specimens of that colour. Wynn found his Russian mastiff surly in disposition, so with true Victorian thoroughness he records how he 'seized him by the collar and beat him with a slipper until tired of beating'. Following this treatment he found the animal's disposition much improved, and it was never again surly to his owner.

The word 'alan' could be of Celtic origin, as I know of at least one example in an ancient Welsh dictionary, where the alan is translated as meaning 'stag' or 'deer'. One wonders whether the animal was some type of staghound, but against this there is the Spanish 'alano' which is very much a mastiff type.

4

A far more likely answer can be found in the late fourteenth century writings of Gaston, third Comte de Foix, more commonly known as Gaston Phoebus. This French nobleman's book on hunting describes the dogs in current use at this time. Amongst the collection he listed the *alan gentil, alan viautre* and *alan de boucherie*.

He remarks that the *alan gentil* are 'they who by their strength and stature can do more harm than any other breed', and later 'alans are prickly, and nasty-tempered although giddier and madder than other kinds of hounds. For a good alan must gallop on like a greyhound and when he has got up to his game, he must let his teeth in and not let go'.

When Edmund de Langley translated the book into English, it was apparent from the text that the alan was well known, as it was unnecessary to describe it. Chaucer mentions the alan, yet when the Laws of Canute were made in 1016 the alan is not mentioned. It can therefore be presumed that it was unknown in England at this time, and was probably introduced by the Normans.

Gaston Phoebus describes another hunting dog as a *mastin*. When Edmond de Langley translated the word he substituted this for 'mastiff' but it is of doubtful accuracy in translation. In records of French boar hunting kennels of the period of Gaston Phoebus there are listed amongst the breeds alaunts, mastins, and grandes dogues anglais; the latter are much more likely to be related to our modern mastiff.

In many of the above references, the alan is listed as being distinct from the mastiff, but we can neither prove, nor disprove that there was cross-breeding between them. What we must take into account is that in these early times, as today, the word 'hound' was loosely applied to anything as different as a basset and a great dane. It is a mistake to adhere too rigidly to names as such, so often animals of a diversity of type were called by the same name.

Saxon References

Returning to the mastiff and its predecessors in England, the Saxons seem to have given the breed a name which persisted well into the eighteenth century, the 'bandog'. From various descriptions, one presumes that the old British *pugnax* had been renamed due to the habit of using it as a watchdog, thus chained (*banda* – a Saxon word for chain). It was common practice to tie the dog by day, but to release him at night to enable him to carry out his guard duties. The obvious inference is that the bandog was a watchdog, or guard-dog, but whether a specific, and recognisable breed, or whether a name given to any chained guard-dog, is not clear. ·

The Board of Celtic Studies of the University of Wales have been of considerable assistance in my historical research. The twelfth century Welsh word *costog* was used to describe a mastiff, house-dog, watchdog, bandog, cur, or mongrel. This shows how much value can be attached to such a name. The bandog was not particularly valuable, as witness the Ancient Laws of Wales (circa 1250): *costog kyn boet brenhim bieffo ny thal eithyr keinhawc cotta* (a costog, although it is a king who shall own it, is of no more value than four curt pence). It was a spirited animal, however, as in the *Cymdeithas Llên Cymru*, we read *ai*

5

costog oi emul oi anos pan fyno (with a dog at his side to set on at will) – the reference is to a shepherd.

The Welsh adjective *costogaidd* can be used to describe a surly, or churlish disposition, and Sir Ifor Williams has an interesting note on the word in the Bulletin of the Board of Celtic Studies. He writes '. . . the costog earned a bad reputation I know very well, but I do not believe that it is quite as bad as it appears to be in the Welsh Laws. It appears to me that the animal was essentially a watch-dog. It was easy for such a dog, by faithfully keeping watch, to earn a bad reputation. Its task were not exactly to welcome anyone . . .'.

The other ancient Welsh word applied to the breed was *gafaelgi* (from *gafael* – to hold, to grip). The word has been translated as being mastiff, or bulldog, which suggests that these breeds were similar at about this period. In the *White Book Mabiniog* of the thirteenth century, we read *gavaelgikydenawc ach y law* (at his (the shepherd's) side, a shaggy mastiff). In the fifteenth century there is another reference: *beth a dalan deucan ci o filgwn heb gafaelgi* (what good are greyhounds, two hundred of them without a gafaelgi). Again, 'the *gafaelgi* takes fierce hold of the stag's throat, and is black in colour'.

These extracts help to verify what I have already outlined, that several types existed, all of one family group. Their uses ranged from shepherd's watchdog, a shaggy mastiff, and the type of animal which possessed the bulldog's habit of attacking the head, or throat. That the type was of value is demonstrated by the quotation of its being of more use than two hundred greyhounds. In recent times, the word *gafaelgi* is given as meaning mastiff in Richard's dictionary of 1753, but in Walters' dictionary of 1771 it is translated as bulldog. In the Llanstephan MS 189 (1772) the term *costog-ast* is translated as 'band bitch'. The other Welsh word which is of significance is *costowci* but it is very wide in use, and translation. It has been translated as meaning mastiff, cur, mongrel and bulldog, and was also used figuratively to describe a surly, or morose person.

One of the most authoritative sources of information about dogs in ancient Wales is in the laws of Howel the Good. Howel died in 950 AD and it is presumed that the laws attributed to him were written in the eleventh century. There are certain passages which are of significance to mastiff history. I quote from Howel.

'There are three kinds of curs, the mastiff, the shepherd dog, and the house dog.' It may be presumed that the dog of this period was essentially a working animal, used in much the same way as some of the foreign mastiffs today, guarding flocks, watching for wolves, and keeping human marauders at bay.

The Norman Era

In the Norman era there is supposed to have been a mastiff type, an example of which is depicted on the famous Bayeaux tapestry showing King Harold with hawk and hound. Some consider the larger hounds to be mastiffs, but in my opinion the dogs are built on far too racy lines for the mastiff even of that period, and are probably the hunting *alan* of Gaston Phoebus' description. It is only in the reign of Henry II that we find the word mastiff being used specifically. This would suggest that it was probably Norman in origin, and derived from the Latin *massivus* (massive) suggesting an animal of some substance.

The Forest Laws of Henry III make reference to the mastiff: 'and therefore farmers and substantial freeholders dwelling within the forest, may keep mastiffs for the defence of their homes within the same, provided that such mastiffs be expeditated according to the laws of the forest. The way of expeditating mastiffs is done after this manner. Three claws of the fore feet shall be cut off by the skin by setting one of the forefeet upon a piece of wood, eight inches thick and a foot square and, with a mallet setting a chisel of two or three inches broad upon the claws of the forefeet, and at one blow cutting them clean off. And this expeditating (by some called hambling, or lawing of dogs), ought to be enquired of by Regarders of the Forest every third year. And to prevent such as are not expeditated and the owners of them amerced three shillings for keeping such dogs so outlawed'.

It may be some compensation in our regimented form-filling age, to note that the heavy hand of the civil servant was not unknown even in the days of Henry III. An important point emerges from these laws. The Regarder was paid sixty silver shillings, supplied with a horse yearly, plus a lance and shield. As there were only sixteen such officers in Britain, it was obviously an important office.

The basic idea of treating the mastiff to this barbarism was to render it incapable of pulling down the Royal deer. What was this mastiff so fleet of foot that unless expeditated could chase and pull down a deer? Certainly not today's conception of the breed.

As with all laws, exceptions to expeditating were given. If the property of a prince of royal blood, mastiffs were exempted as were other breeds of dog, but one sentence is of particular historical significance. It reads 'no other dogges are to be expeditated but mastives and such curres that are of the mastive kind'.

Obviously the mastiff was of several kinds during this period. Were the 'kinds' assessed on size, or how did they differ from the mastiff proper? We can only guess. That the 'kinds' were strong and capable dogs is proven by the need to expeditate them. Could there have been a proportional size difference such as exists today between the Mastiff and Bullmastiff?

2

The Mastiffs of the Tudor and Stuart Era

The most famous of all mastiff stories, which every mastiff owner today is proud to relate, comes from the period of Henry V. It tells how, at the battle of Agincourt Sir Piers Legh, a knight at Arms to King Henry, fell in the battle, and was guarded by his favourite mastiff bitch. Sir Piers died of his wounds, but the bitch was returned to England and established the Lyme Hall strain of mastiffs. We shall look at the story in more detail in the chapter on Lyme Hall.

The Tudor era has a special significance in mastiff history, due to the references made to the breed in various accounts of bull and bear baiting. One can so easily romanticise the period of the first Queen Elizabeth. A love song by Dowland, or a courtly pavan played on the virginals may epitomise the culture of the Elizabethan Court, but human life was not sacrosanct, and cruelty to animals was commonplace. Perhaps the red hair may have given an outward indication of the fire within this great Tudor monarch, but the heart-shaped face and bejewelled femininity of her court dress gave no indication of her very unfeminine love of cruelty in blood sports – nor of the perspicacity of this amazing woman in affairs of state. The morbid brutality towards animals in these times is an indictment of our forebears, although one realises that life for the lower orders must have been soul-destroying, and any diversion was likely to be enthusiastically followed by the mob.

Bear-baiting became almost a national sport, and Elizabeth enjoyed the sordid spectacle as much as did those dregs of society who frequented the bear gardens. Paris Garden in Southwark was a notorious centre for bear baiting, and it was probably there that Shakespeare became acquainted with the sport; hence his references to the bears in several plays. The most graphic account of the bear garden comes from the pen of Thomas Dekker who in 1596 wrote:

> Sometimes a roar would echo through the streets from the bear garden, that filthy hell where devils from the slums torture the helpless. The very noise of that place put me in the mind of hell. The bear dragt to the stake, showed like a black rugged soul that was damned, and newly committed to the infernal churle, the dogs like so many devils inflicting torments upon it. At length a blind bear was tied to the stake, and instead of baiting him with dogs, a company of creatures that had the shapes of men, and the faces of Christians, took office of beadles upon them and whipped Mr Hunks till the blood ran down his old shoulders. It was some sport to see innocence triumph over tyranny by beholding those unnecessary tormentors to go away with scratched hands, or torn legs for the beast armed only by nature to defend himself against violence.

One can only agree with Dame Edith Sitwell when she commented on the above in her *Fanfare for Elizabeth*: '. . . one would like to think that those scratched by the blind bear died after suffering the tortures of gangrene; perhaps they did. . . . I hope so'. (Dame Edith was, incidentally, a great dog lover and the family once owned a pair of mastiffs which were described as 'like a pair of tawny lions'.)

Dekker's opinion of the bear garden was echoed by Lupton who in 1632 wrote of Paris Garden 'This may better be termed a foul den than a fair garden. Here come few who either regard their credit or loss of time. The swaggering roarer, the bloudy butcher, the cunning cheater, the rotten bawd, the swearing drunkards have their rendezvous here.'

The normal procedure at a bear bait was to have the muzzled bear tied to a stake by a length of rope or chain, forty feet usually being considered to be the correct length. The baiting dogs were arranged around the arena, and when the bear was unmuzzled the dogs were released, usually in pairs. The normal mode of attack was by hurling themselves against the bear in the hope of over-balancing it with a spring at the throat. Protective collars were not normally worn by the dogs, so the jaws of the bear were lethal, his claws punishing in the extreme, but his hug was usually fatal. The picture on p. 10 shows bear baiting, but the proportionate size of dog and bear may not be correct.

It is difficult to establish exactly who owned the baiting dogs. There is proof that buildings called 'the dog house' existed in convenient propinquity to the bear garden, but the ownership of the dogs, or bears, has not, to my knowledge, been recorded. It could well be that the sporting gentry of the times owned both animals, thus creating the dual purpose of providing sport, and at the same time, a wager on the chances of survival. In letters patent of 1620, Edward Alleyn was styled as 'master of bears and dogs' at the Royal Bear Garden on the Bankside in Southwark, suggesting that this was an official post.

The crucial question which arises from the numerous references of baitings in the Tudor era was whether or not the dogs were mastiffs. Within the loosely defined terms of the period, I would say that they were, but I am equally certain that they would not be recognisable as such today.

The very mechanics of baiting would require an agile, but thick set, heavy dog, since if the bear could be toppled at the first onslaught his chances of survival were considerably reduced.

A narrow, lightly built animal would be at a considerable disadvantage, and weight and substance must have been of primary importance. Hertsner, writing of baiting in 1598, states '. . . there is a place built in the form of a theatre which serves for the baiting of bulls, and bears. They are fastened behind and worried by great English bulldogs'. The reference was to a Bankside theatre.

As far as I am aware, no drawing or painting exists of the modern mastiff-type dog baiting a bull in a Tudor bullring or bear garden. The nearest thing to a true representation is Goya's etching 'Dogs baiting a bull' from his *Tauromaquia* series in the British Museum. Goya was, of course, working much later, at the end of the eighteenth century. Goya's dogs look very like the

'*Mastiffs Baiting a Bear.*' *Richard Pynson, 1521. One must accept a degree of artistic licence in a drawing of this period but the baiting dogs appear to be half as large as the bear itself.*

modern bullmastiff whilst most English baiting prints which I have studied depict dogs of a decidedly 'boxer' type, although we must take into consideration the fact that the present-day bulldog only remotely resembles the animal of even one hundred and fifty years ago.

Wynn had doubts about the participation of mastiffs in baiting, and half-heartedly suggests in his book (p. 128):

> It will readily be seen that for baiting purposes, while size in the mastiff meant power, at the same time mere size without proportionate muscular development and bulk with the characteristic short head, and powerful jaws was not the standard aimed at then, or to be aimed at now. Some otherwise fair judges have fallen into the error of considering size an essential in the mastiff, and have mistaken true mastiff type, preferring the more extenuated type derived from a Boarhound or Great Danish cross.

Bull baiting enjoyed nationwide popularity, with the centres of activity in London and the Midlands. It is alleged to have started in 1204 when Lord Stamford of Lincolnshire witnessed a pair of butcher's dogs tormenting a bull. This so appealed to him that space was offered on his estate to establish the sport of bull baiting. The bull was tethered by a heavy chain, and, according to reports of baitings, an experienced bull would occasionally dig a hollow with his fore-feet in which he would place his nose, knowing this to be the most vulnerable to attack.

Amongst the galaxy of talent which appeared in the era was Dr John Kay (1510–1573) a physician of great culture, who chose to Latinise his name to 'Dr Caius' in his many writings. He will long be remembered for the generous endowment of the Cambridge College which still bears his name. A great naturalist himself, he wrote a treatise on British dogs addressed to his friend Gesner. This was in Latin; it was later translated into English and published in this country. The mastiff was described as 'vast, huge, stubborn, eager, of a heavy and burdenous body, and therefore but of little swiftness'. Caius was aware of the existence of more than one type of mastiff as he referred to dogs being 'of the greater and weightier sort used for drawing water by being placed in a tread mill, or as a baggage dog to transport the tools of tinkers', yet another instance of both the types present within the group loosely called 'mastiff' and the variety of duties to which these animals were placed, guarding, carrying, baiting and fighting were all part of their lot.

This is substantiated by William Harrison whose *Description of England* written in 1587 describes life in rural England, the state of agriculture, customs, pastimes and natural history of the country. You will observe that Harrison was not exactly unaware of Caius' writings, and could well have adapted these into his chronicles. Harrison's opening sentence is far nearer to the truth than the words of many of his successors.

> Dogs of the homely kind are either shepherd's curs, or mastiffs. The first are so common that it need not be spoken of. Wherefore I will leave this cur unto his own kind, and go hand in hand with the mastiff, tiedog, or bandog, so called because many are tied up in chains and strong bands in day-time from doing hurt abroad. It is a huge dog, stubborn, ugly, eager, burdenous of body and therefore

11

of but little swiftness, and fearful to behold and oftentimes more fierce and fell than any Arcdian cur. Our Englishmen to the intent that these dogs may be more cruel and fierce, assist nature with some art, use, and custom. For although this dog is capable of courage, voilent, valiant stout and bold, yet will they increase their stomachs (bravery) by teaching them to bait the bear, the bull, the lion, and such like cruel and bloody beasts (either brought over, or kept at home for that purpose), without any collar to protect their throats. Oftentimes thereto, they train them up in fighting and wrestling with a man (having for the safeguard of his life either a pikestaff, club, sword, or privy coat*, whereby they become more fierce and cruel unto strangers.

I say that of mastiffs some bark only, with fierce and open mouth, but will not bite. Some do both bark, and bite. But the cruelist do either not bark at all, or bite before they bark and therefore to be more feared than the other. The force which is in them surmounteth all belief, and the fast hold which they take with their teeth exceeds all credit, for three of them against a bear, four against a lion, are sufficient to try masteries with them. Some of our mastiffs will rage only at nightime, some are to be tied up both day and night. Such also are suffered to go loose about the house and yard, are so gentle in the daytime that children may ride on their backs and play with them at their pleasures. Divers of them likewise are of such jealousy over their master and whatsoever of his household, that if a stranger do embrace, or touch any of them, they will fall fiercely upon them unto their extreme mischief if their fury be not prevented.

Harrison's observations may be considered authentic, but I would draw attention to the opening paragraph in which the mastiff is described as 'of the homely kind'. So much nonsense has been written of the rarity of the breed, and its association with England's stately homes. Harrison states quite clearly that the dog was not the highly prized animal which some have chosen to consider it, but was, in every sense, a working dog.

When the Bankside playhouses were not being used for plays, baiting spectacles seemed to have been the alternative form of amusement. This is probably why Shakespeare knew of the mastiff, and could even have known the Sir Piers Legh story, when, in Henry V (Act 3, scene 7) he wrote:

Rambures: That island of England breeds very valiant creatures, their mastiffs are of unmatchable courage.
Orleans: Foolish curs that run winking into the mouth of a Russian bear and have their heads crushed like rotten apples. You may as well say that's a valiant flea that dare eat his breakfast on the lip of a lion.
French Constable: Just, just, and the men do sympathise with the mastiffs in robustious and rough coming on, leaving their wits with their wives, and then they give them great meals of beef, and iron, and steel, they will eat like wolves, and fight like devils.

Shakespeare was aware of the mastiff courage, but had a poor opinion of its intelligence, as the above is not an isolated one suggesting that the breed was a demon fighter, but lacked intelligence:

Clifford: Are these thy bears? We'll bait thy bears to death,
And manacle the bearward in their chains.
Richard Plantagenet: Oft have I seen a hot o'erweening cur

* A coat of mail worn under the ordinary garments.

12

> Run back and bite, because he was witheld:
> Who, being suffered, with the bear's fell paw,
> Hath clapped his tail between his legs and cried;
> And such a piece of service will you do,
> If you oppose yourselves to match Lord Warwick.
> (Henry VI part 2, Act 5, scene 1, line 148)

Here the mastiff is not named as such, but the bear baiting would suggest a mastiff. In Troilus and Cressida, Shakespeare makes further comment on the mastiff's love of combat (Act 1, scene 3, line 391):

> Two curs shall tame each other, pride alone
> Must tarre the mastiffs on, as t'were their bone.

Memories of the Bankside bear gardens are reflected in 'The Merry Wives of Windsor' (Act 1, scene 2, lines 260–272):

> *Slender*: Why do your dogs bark so? Be there bears in the town?
> *Anne*: I think there are sir; I heard them talk'd of.
> *Slender*: I love the sport well; but I shall as soon quarrel at it as any man in England. You are afraid, if you see the bear loose, are you not?
> *Anne*: Ay, indeed sir.
> *Slender*: That's meat and drink to me now, I have seen Sackerson loose twenty times, and have taken him by the chain; But, I warrant you, the women have so cried and shriek'd at it that it pass'd; but women, indeed, cannot abide 'em, they are very ill favour'd rough things.

The final, and most descriptive account of the mastiff of the era is from Conrad Heresbach, 'newly Englished by Barnaby Googe, London 1586'.

> In choosing a mastie that keepth the house you must provide such a one as hath a large, mightie body, a great shrill voice, that both with his barking – yea, being not seen, with the horror of his voice, put him to flight. His stature must neither be long nor short, but well set. His head great, his eyes sharp and fierce, either brown, or grey. His lips blackish, neither turning up, nor hanging too much downe. His mouth blacke, and wide, his neather jaw fat, and coming out of it on either side a fang appearing more outward than his other teeth, his upper teeth even with his neather, not hanging too much over, sharpe, and hidden with his lips. His countenace like a lion's, his breast great and shag haired, his shoulders broad, his legs big, his tail short, his feet very great. His disposition must neither be too gentle not too curst, that he neither fawn upon a thief, nor fly upon his friends. Very waking, no gadder abroad, nor lavish of his mouth, barking without cause. It maketh no matter that he be not swift, for he is but to fight at home and give warning of the enemy. A black dog is best, because of the hurt he may do to the thief by reason of not being seen.

When one considers that this description was made four hundred years ago, it is still remarkably accurate as a breed standard. I am not suggesting that it completely describes the requirements of the modern show mastiff, but the characteristics of the mastiff group as a whole are embodied in the description. As I write, my pack are 'raising their shrill voices' in one of their nocturnal howlings, making me thankful of the comparative isolation of this house, as surely neighbours would be 'put to flight by the horror of their voices'.

The significant feature in the description is the 'fat neather jaw' and it cannot be coincidence that the same description was mentioned of the old British pugnace of Roman times.

The Stuart Period

The most important document of this period is the famous Van Dyck portrait of the children of Charles I, a good copy of which may be seen in the National Portrait Gallery of London, the original being in the collection of H.M. The Queen.

The dog is somewhat coarse, with cropped ears, and although a trifle houndy in head, has immense breadth to his skull. This can be gauged by comparison with the size of the boy's hand, which is placed on it. The boy is, of course, the future Charles II.

The white blaze which runs up the foreface of the dog is not unusual for mastiff types of this period. In fact, these white markings were common well into the nineteenth century. It may be coincidence that Van Dyck portrayed a very similar dog to the one in the Royal collection when painting his portrait of Thomas Killigrew, which also hangs in the National Portrait Gallery. The likeness is so close that one wonders whether this dog was known to the artist and borrowed for portraiture.

Charles I was a great dog lover, and even advertised for his 'bobtailed black mastiff' when the animal had gone astray.

The Eighteenth Century

There are a number of eighteenth century portraits of owners with their mastiffs, and whilst we must not presume that each typified the breed of the period, the greater proportion show parti-coloured dogs with long heads (as in the van Dyck portrait). Sir Godfrey Kneller (1646–1723) portrayed such a dog in his painting of Charles Bowles of Cleaver (1704–1780). Allan Ramsay (1713–1784) painted a tall, heavily built, parti-coloured mastiff in his portrait of Charles Edward Louis Casimir, 'The Young Pretender'. One could perhaps allow for artist's licence, but the dog's head is over waist high at the side of his owner, and the animal carries his tail in a sweeping curve over his back. Richard Conway (1740–1821) in his portrait of Master Thornton seems to have recaptured not only the appearance of van Dyck's dog, but the position of the young owner's left hand on the dog's head.

The animal is crop-eared and the whole portrait so like the van Dyck that one wonders whether the artist was commissioned to paint the picture in the royal manner.

Count Buffon, in his *Historie Naturelle* of 1755 illustrated several mastiff types, including 'Le Dogue de Forte Race', a not so houndy and broader-skulled type of parti-coloured black and white dog.

A famous mastiff was owned by David Garrick (1717–1779), the well known actor manager. Garrick, always a dog lover, was particularly upset at the death of a favourite spaniel, and replaced it with a mastiff, which he called Dragon.

van Dyck: The Five Eldest Children of Charles I.
Reproduced by gracious permission of Her Majesty The Queen.

Dragon lived at the Garrick residence at Hampton, but once appeared on the stage at Drury Lane, and was later painted by the fashionable portrait painter Zoffany. This shows Dragon in the foreground of a painting of the Garrick family in front of the Shakespeare's Temple at Hampton. A long headed type again, he appears to have been a light fawn in colour, and definitely had a black mask. Dragon survived his master; in fact Mrs Garrick was distressed by the excitment which the dog showed when his deceased master's carriage arrived at Hampton, and the animal expected his customary caress. The carriage on this occasion contained Mrs Garrick, and her close friend Hannah More. Dragon must have taken his guard duties seriously as Hannah More wrote an ode to the dog on which he is described as:

> Dragon, thou tyrant of the yard,
> Great namesake of that furious guard
> That watch'd of the fruits Hesperian.

The ode is a very lengthy one, and Hannah More, whose abilities at writing plays were in no way comparable to her admiration of Garrick, sent this ode, and her play *Percy* to Garrick together with 'a jar of codlings done in Indian pickle'. It is not recorded if Garrick favoured the codlings, but he certainly

15

van Dyck: Thomas Killigrew and his dog, Chatsworth Courtauld Institute of Art.

found little favour with the play. His influence as manager of Drury Lane was then in decline, and it would have been improbable that he could have helped his devotee.

One of the most quoted mastiff engravings of the late eighteenth century was that of Thomas Bewick which appeared in the author's *General History of Quadrupeds*. Bewick was born in 1753 in Northumberland, and became England's most famous wood engraver, and author of those wonderful scenes of rural England which frequently conclude the chapters of books of that period. In 1785 he began to make the woodcuts for his book which was published at the turn of the century, and followed in 1804 by two volumes of his *History of British Birds*.

Bewick began his working life as an engraver of silver, and Audubon writing of him in later life described him as a 'perfect old Englishman who worked in a soiled nightcap, and slept at night wrapped in a blanket on the floor'. He died at the age of 75 and was buried at Ovingham churchyard just across the river from the house in which he was born.

This brief biography shows that old engraver hardly moved out of his native parish, and whilst he had the true countryman's ability to appreciate and translate the changes of nature which surrounded him, it was necessary for him to copy from other engravers any subjects with which he was not intimately acquainted. Bewick's much debated mastiff was not taken from life, but is a direct copy of Buffon's mastiff of a half century earlier. Bewick drew his mastiff looking left, whilst Buffon's looks right, but the dogs are identical, even to the black markings. The mastiff of the period has so often been considered to be as portrayed by these two illustrators, but this shows that there was but one illustrator, the other copying an existing engraving.

Howitt, another engraver working in the early nineteenth century has given us several pictures of mastiffs. In his 'bull with mastiff' the unfortunate animal impaled upon the bull's horn appears to be about the size of the modern Airedale Terrier, rough-coated, and considerably marked with white, yet the same artist's picture of dogs at a bear baiting are distinctly bulldoggy, short on the leg, and broad of chest. A further variation exists in the same artist's 'mastiff with spaniel' where a somewhat coarse, crop-eared animal with a strong muzzle looks threateningly at the spaniel. This latter mastiff could have been one of the so called 'farm mastiffs' which several writers have mentioned, including Wynn, who considered them to be a cross between the mastiff and sheep dog.

To illustrate just how loosely the name mastiff was applied, a picture of a well known mastiff called 'Lion' is reproduced on page 19. Compare Lion with the bear-baiting mastiffs of Howitt, or Bewick's mastiff, and the resemblance is scant.

It was about this time, namely the nineteenth century, that many were bemoaning the fact that the mastiff 'in its purity' was almost extinct. Bewick in his *History of Quadrupeds* wrote 'the mastiff in his pure and unmixed state is seldom to be met with'. The generality of dogs by that name seem to be compounded of the bulldog, Danish Mastiff and bandog. (This is interesting as Bewick does not consider the word mastiff and bandog to be synonymous.)

Bewick's illustration of mastiff and bulldog, published in 1816.

Howitt's 'Bull and Mastiff'. Published 1810. The dog is parti coloured, and appears to be the size of an Airedale.

Lion. Drawn by Rev. Cooper Williams from the original in the possession of Powell Snell, Esq.

Sydenham Edwards in his *Cynographia Brittanica* (1800) says much the same thing, whilst William Taplin in *The Sportsmans Cabinet* (1803) states that the breed has been 'materially reduced by various intermixtures and experimental crosses' so that the dog of that time 'in its uncontaminated state is rarely seen'. He later mentions that the mastiff came in a variety of sizes and colours, but that the pure breed was difficult to obtain. John Scott in *The Sportsmans Repository* (1820) states that the breed 'in a pure state is no longer to be found among us', and in fact this appears to have been the opinion of most writers up to the first quarter of the nineteenth century.

The question which I pose is whether the mastiff 'in its purity' ever existed. Obviously one person's conception was totally different from that of another. There were no recorded pedigrees, and travel in Britain, as in any other country, was laboriously slow. It is extremely unlikely that persons from the South or the West Country ever saw dogs from Cheshire or Yorkshire, and it is safe to assume that with the local pockets of breeding, a degree of inbreeding was practiced, which may have given local uniformity of type. That Howitt's bear-baiting mastiffs look like bull-baiting types of the period cannot be denied, and to quote the late Dr Joad 'it all depends on what you mean by mastiff'.

There are two paintings which I think summarise average mastiffs of the early nineteenth century. The first is by Gilpin and reproduced on page 21. He is a large, majestic broad skulled, black and white animal with tremendous depth of body, and relatively short limbs. The strength of shoulders suggests a dog of great power, and judging by the width across his muzzle, this dog possessed a good grip and broad under-jaw. The second painting is of a somewhat similar animal. The original was purchased at Sotheby's, by its present owner, Mr Ivan Monosori, who recognised the dog as being the mastiff used in an engraving by Reinagle, and which had previously been considered as being by that artist. Sotheby's attribute the painting to William Marlow (1740–1813), and as the dog is chained at a wharfside saw-mill with St Paul's in the background, one presumes that the mill was probably at Southwark. This was Marlow's birthplace. He spent most of his life in London and painted both Blackfriars Bridge and St Paul's on other occasions. The middle distance and background of Mr Monostori's painting are suggestive of Marlow's style. The engraver Reinagle was a contemporary of Marlow, surviving him by two years. Although better known as an engraver, Reinagle was a fine animal painter in his earlier years.

The dog in the painting shows definite mastiff characteristics. There is the white about the head common in the breed at this time. The muzzle is broad, with sufficient flew. There appears to be good width between the ears, the loin is slightly arched, and the hindquarters well muscled as are the shoulders of what is obviously a working dog. On the back of the painting some writer has recorded that the dog is of the Lyme Hall strain. If nothing else, this proves the notoriety of Lyme Hall despite the criticisms later made of dogs of the strain.

So we approach the period when mastiffs and mastiff breeding become something more than supposition. In the survey so far, the recurrent theme

The Duke of Hamilton's Mastiff and Greyhounds. Oil painting by Sawrey Gilpin, 1780.

'The Mastiff' (from 'The Sportsman's Cabinet' 1803) by P. Reinagle. Probably engraved by Reinagle from painting by Marlow (see text).

21

has been that all sorts of animals were classified as 'mastiffs'. If there was ever a 'pure state' as the old writers call it, why was it necessary to cross, and recross such mastiffs? Even in such establishments as Lyme Hall some suggest that outcrosses were necessary, but it was only at such places that a pure line of mastiffs existed.

We can safely assume that mastiffs were kept as guards in stately homes, but we must also realise that there were tinkers' baggage dogs called mastiffs, butchers' mastiffs, farm mastiffs, and many others of doubtful parentage. It was from this heterogeneous collection, plus the use of certain foreign breeds, that the mastiff as we shall consider it in the next chapter, was evolved.

3

Early Recorded History

There are several figures who dominated early mastiff breeding and to whom scant credit has been given in the past. The first of these early enthusiasts was Bill George of Canine Castle, Kensal Green, London. He had been a butcher's boy in early life, but had later managed to buy from the widow of Ben White an established dog breeding business. Ben White had dealt mainly in baiting and fighting dogs, calling his establishment 'May Tree Cottage': Bill George created his 'Canine Castle' on this site.

Bill George had a worldwide reputation as one of the most honest and sporting of persons in the dog trade, and as a supplier of bulldogs he would often entertain the sporting bucks of the era with demonstrations of the courage and abilities of his strain. He named foreign royalty amongst his clients, and even Charles Dickens visited him on more than one occasion. It is probable that the character of Bill Sykes' bulldog was based on a Canine Castle inmate. The magazine *Punch* published a cartoon of Bill in his establishment entitled 'Mr Punch's visit to a most remarkable place'.

A letter was once addressed to him as 'Bill George, Devil's Castle, Bloodhound Corner, Tyke Lane, London'. It reached its destination. His pride was hurt when on one occasion a letter addressed to 'Mr Bill George, Dog Fancier, London' was returned to the sender as being insufficiently addressed. Bill enquired of the identity of the Postmaster General, and on being told that it was Lord John Manners he replied: 'Then you can tell the Post Office fools that if his Lordship don't know me, I don't know manners'. It is difficult to believe that this most famous and important dog dealer is almost forgotten today, and few seem to credit him for his development both of bulldog and mastiff. He also bred 'Toy Bulldogs', most of which were exported to France where there was an ever increasing demand. This is probably the foundation from which the French Bulldog evolved.

Bill was no intellectual, and some of his associates were of questionable repute, yet he was respected by all who came in contact with him, despite the roughness of his exterior. He died at the age of 79, not apparently a very wealthy man. Dog shows were then beginning to make themselves felt, and tended to kill his much more utilitarian conception of the game. It is a rather sad postscript to read in *The Kennel Chronicle* of August 1884 that a fund was to be raised to provide for his widow. I quote from the notice.

Bill George of Canine Castle, Kensal New Town died recently. He was a character in his day and generation. He is described by one who knew him well as a sturdy,

23

PUNCH'S VISIT TO A VERY REMARKABLE PLACE

'Punch's Visit to a Very Remarkable Place.' This drawing first appeared in Punch *in 1846. It shows Mr Punch with Bill George surrounded by his kennel of bulldogs. It is interesting to note that although forgotten today, Bill George was of sufficient interest in his era to merit such a cartoon.*

straightforward, honest dealing man, and known to be trustworthy by all who came in contact with him. Bill George maintained an honourable name in business which abounded with temptations. He was buried at Kensal Green on 9 June 1881.

In 1884 the same publication records:

During the last few years of his life Bill George was jilted to some extent by Dame Fortune, and hence his widow who is paralysed is totally unprovided for, and has no resources. A subscription list has been drawn up, and the Editor of 'Sporting Life' will receive contributions.

I hope that the world was as sporting to the widow as Bill had been to the dog fraternity. Throughout his life he kept mastiffs, and was always on the lookout for anything large, handsome, and courageous, likely to catch a client's eye. He kept few records, or if he did they perished with him, but he was a major contributor in the evolution of the mastiff and has to date been completely overlooked.

Nineteenth Century Mastiffs

For an account of early recorded mastiff breeding we need to concentrate on comparatively few names. Bill George, J. W. Thompson, T. H. V. Lukey, Mr E. Hanbury and the Lyme Hall mastiffs. Obviously there were many

The Mastiff.

An illustration used in a Victorian children's book.

The English Mastiff.

'*The Ancient Briton and his Mastiff*', *from a Victorian engraving for a children's book.*

others, but from stock owned or bred by these few pioneers came the funda-
mentals of the modern mastiff type.

We have already glimpsed at Bill George, whom Wynn admired but thought
that 'due to the shortage of space at Canine Castle his mastiffs were not always
well reared, but the faults were of nurture, rather than nature, as they were
rarely passed on'. It must also be appreciated that written pedigrees did not
feature very strongly in the period and that such records that were kept abound
with 'Lions' and 'Tigers' in the males and 'Countess' and 'Duchess' on the
distaff side. I shall in many instances quote the owner's name as a form of
differentiation.

T. H. V. Lukey

Son of a Kentish squire, born in 1804, he became a King Charles Spaniel
fancier at an early age, and it was probably through this breed that he became
known to Bill George and other London dog dealers.

Mr Lukey claimed that his introduction to mastiffs occurred one morning in
the Serpentine, London, when a magnificent black mastiff was being exercised
by a manservant in livery. On enquiring of the dog's owner, he was informed
that it was the property of the Marquis of Hertford. Mr Lukey decided to call
on the Marquis and enquire whether the animal could be used at stud.

One pictures the scene in those days of social protocol when even a squire's
son would have been considered rather impudent in making such a request.
The Marquis was not unsympathetic but asked Mr Lukey what bitch he
proposed breeding from. The reply from Mr Lukey was that he was not at
present a mastiff owner, but that he would obtain a suitable bitch if the
Marquis would allow her to be mated to his dog. This was favourably received,
with the stipulation that final consent would only be given if the bitch in
question met the necessary standard. Thus Mr Lukey made his first purchase.
It was from George White, a well-known dealer. She was a cropped-eared,
bob-tailed brindle for which Mr Lukey paid forty pounds, with the proviso
that White had a puppy back in due course. The bitch was of unknown
parentage; in fact, like the Marquis's Pluto she need not have been a mastiff at
all, though White considered her to be an 'Alpine Mastiff'. When the Marquis
was confronted with the bitch he asked 'Did you steal her, and mutilate her to
prevent recognition?' Mr Lukey assured him that she was honestly procured so
the request to use Pluto at stud was granted, on the condition that the Marquis
had a puppy from the litter if there was one which he fancied. Two brindled
pups came from the mating. One was offered to the Marquis but was declined,
the other went back to White as agreed. Lukey retained the pup which he
called 'Yarrow' and resold the dam to George White for the same price which
he had paid for her. Thus Mr Lukey obtained his foundation stock, which was
almost certainly foreign in origin, and probably contained no English mastiff
blood whatsoever.

When Yarrow became adult she was mated to Couchez sometimes called Turk
who was the property of George White, and later sold to Lord Waldegrave.
The breeding of Couchez is shrouded in mystery. He was certainly a fighting

dog and undoubtedly imported; he was not as large as Pluto, and red smut in colour. Some considered him a smooth Alpine mastiff but Wynn thought him to be a Spanish Bull Mastiff. White always maintained that he was imported from Italy. He was barely thirty inches at the shoulder and weighed one hundred and thirty pounds, but pitted against much larger dogs, he was never beaten. From the Couchez/Yarrow mating Mr Lukey retained Bruce 1, a dark brindle with an almost black head and white stripe running up over the face. Bruce 2 was also out of Yarrow, but from a later litter sired by another mastiff which White had at the time, which was also of unknown parentage.

It can be seen that the foundation of Mr Lukey's kennel was not English, yet it was a strain which ran in many mastiffs of the nineteenth century and therefore presumably through dogs today. Lukey's dogs were extremely large, mostly brindled, but often deficient in muscle and activity.

Mr Lukey died in 1882 having spent the greater part of his life at Locksbottom in Kent. We shall refer to the strain later, but this condensed account proves the foreign element in what has so long been considered to be a truly British dog.

John Crabtree

'Old John Crab' as he was affectionately known to his friends, was a gamekeeper at Kirklees Hall, Yorkshire, the home of Sir George Armitage. He was described as being 'considerably over six feet in height, handsome in face and figure, with the courage of a lion, and the true courtesy of a gentleman'. One gathers that John was not a fancier as such, but was more concerned with the utilitarian angle of dogs, which is what one would have expected from someone of his profession.

He 'caught' his first mastiff in 1819. Having set fox traps on the estate he found a trapped mastiff when checking the night's catch. She was released with some difficulty but little damaged, and getting his belt round her neck she was led back to the Hall. Sir George ordered that she be taken to the gun room and locked up; no one was to be told about her. Years later John Crabtree described her as 'brindle, small in ear, broad chested, with a long low body and a dash of bull blood in her'. No enquiry was ever made for the bitch so she became part of the Kirklees establishment and was named Duchess. Like all bitch owners John Crabtree wanted a litter from her so she was mated to Lion. Lion was sired by a dog from Bold Hall and was therefore most probably of Lyme Hall descent (see note in Lyme Hall section). Puppies born from the mating were given to friends, one to a Mrs Brewer, who kept the public house in Kirklees village. This puppy was called Bet and when adult produced a litter to Waterton's Tiger. Tiger was an Irish import, tall, bob-tailed, with an untypical boarhound appearance. The chances of him being a mastiff are pretty slim, but a puppy called Tiny was retained together with another called Venus. Venus was duly mated to Wynn's Lion, and Crabtree had a puppy called Duchess from the resultant litter. Tiny was later mated to a 'keeper's watch dog' on the estate called Nero who had more than his fair share of bulldog in him, but an important stud force came from this second mating. He was Old Tiger, a white faced fawn of tremendous courage and agility. Crabtree then inbred by putting Old Tiger to Duchess 2 and produced, amongst others, a bitch called Dorah. Her importance lies in the fact that she became the foundation of Mr Thompson's famous mastiff kennels.

From a cursory study of the sketch pedigree of Dorah it will be seen that she was probably more English than most. The questionable animal is Waterton's Tiger, who was probably a boarhound, but Wynn's Lion certainly had English blood, and this is also true of Duchess of fox trap fame. Although both Duchess and Nero carried a bulldog element in their breeding it should be appreciated that at this time there were large bulldogs and small mastiffs so the line of demarcation between the two breeds was somewhat arbitrary.

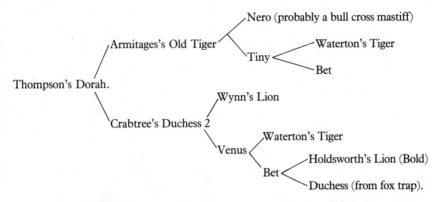

In his utilitarian way John Crabtree bred mastiffs over a long period of time, developing animals of great agility, and soundness of body and temperament these being factors important to him in his conception of the breed as a working guard dog. He died in 1881 at a great age.

I am at a loss to explain the final paragraph of Wynn's very complimentary assessment of this grand old Englishman when he writes: '. . . his idea was to keep, and breed, the pure mastiff of which he prided himself having no idea of crossing with the bulldog'. John Crabtree may have avoided a definite cross, but the so called 'purity' of his mastiff was questionable as the above sketch pedigree shows.

J. W. Thompson (1818–1875)

A Yorkshireman by birth, Mr Thompson purchased his first mastiff from Bill George. She was a brindled bitch called Juno, described by her owner as being 'a good massive type, long in body, but somewhat rugged in coat'. Juno mated to Captain Fenton's Tiger produced Hector, a dog wth a superlative head. His next purchase was from John Crabtree, the bitch called Dorah which we have already mentioned. Dorah mated to Hector produced Lion, who became the property of Sir George Armitage.

In the meanwhile, Mr Thompson had visited the kennels of Mr Lukey and as a result of that visit there began an exchange of bloodlines, so that the activity and soundness of Mr Thompson's strain was usefully married to the size of Mr Lukey's brindles. Mr Thompson's Venus was of Lukey's strain, and mated to Ackroyd's Dan, an old type of mastiff of the Duke of Sutherland's strain produced Thompson's Rose. Thompson mated Rose with Sir Titus Salt's Lion thus going back to his old strain, and produced the important brindle called 'Bill George's Tiger' (stud book number 2345) an animal of immense importance in registered mastiff breeding.

Tiger was given to Bill George when a puppy in appreciation of the many favours which the old dealer had given to Mr Thompson. Tiger became the transmitter not only of the modern head type, but also the activity lacking in many of Mr Lukey's dogs. Tiger was not straight in the foreleg, but never passed the defect on and many of his progeny were active even into extreme old age, an account being given of one son who could at the age of eight, clear a five-barred gate. Like many of Mr Thompson's dogs he was not vast, but one must bear in mind that Mr Thompson publicly stated that '. . . a dog standing thirty inches, head marking twenty-six inches, or twenty-seven inches, and proportionate frame, strong, and active on his legs, would be the height of my ambition'.

Mr E. Hanbury

His residence was Eastrop Grange, Highworth, Wilts: and he became interested in the breed about 1858 when he acquired a bitch called Empress who was by Ansdell's Leo (a Lyme Hall dog) out of Countess. Ansdell was an important animal artist at this time, and several of his paintings are extant. One is of a long-coated mastiff now in Liverpool Art Gallery but a much more important painting is his 'Mastiff and poacher'. This is now in the Marie Moore collection in the USA. It is a particularly fine painting, the dog who is attacking the poacher is a brindle of easily recognisable mastiff type. Ansdell had managed to acquire stock from Lyme Hall which is unusual as the family were not keen on selling their strain. Many mastiffs of the period, some of obscure breeding became conveniently labelled as 'Lyme Hall dogs', and the early stud books record some as 'reputedly Lyme Hall'. Kingdon and Ansdell owned mastiffs which were undisputedly from the Legh residence.

Hanbury's Empress mated to Bill George's Tiger produced a grand headed bitch called Duchess (2365). A feature of her head was an unusually short and blunt foreface. Duchess became a very successful show winner between 1863 and 1865 which not only established Mr Hanbury as a fancier, but encouraged his further breeding with a short foreface as his aim. Duchess mated to Lukey's Governor produced Prince (2326) who although himself reverting back to Lukey's long muzzled type, must have carried the short foreface genetically.

If I may digress at this point, it is important to realise that up until this time most mastiffs were long muzzled though not necessarily narrow skulled. It was something of an innovation to have the shortened foreface although it was precisely this which Wynn had long advocated as being typical.

Prince was mated to Rowe's Nell (a litter sister to Ch. King), a bitch who always threw short heads; they produced Griffin a fine headed fawn and sire of Rajah (2333). Rajah is another of those animals whose influence has had scant recognition. Rajah and Phillis (2394), the latter a brindled granddaughter of Bill George's Tiger, were the two most important animals owned by Mr Hanbury and the progenitors of many of the breed's mainstays that appeared at the turn of the century.

Mr Hanbury's other breeding distinction was the production of Wolsey (5315) to whom many brindles could be traced back. A fine colour plate of this dog appears in Vero Shaw's classic *The Book of the Dog*. Wolsey was by Rajah out of Queen, a brindle who inherited her colour from Phillis. The sire of Phillis was Pemberton's Wolf a brindled son of Bill George's Tiger.

By the early 1870s mastiffs had become one of the numerically strong breeds in the show ring. Sixty-four dogs appeared at Crystal Palace in 1871, and at Curzon Hall, Birmingham, in the same year the mastiffs had the largest class entry of the non-sporting breeds. This trend continued for the next decade with keen competition among such exhibitors as Miss Aglionby, Rev. Mellor, Kingdon, Wynn, Hanbury and Nicholls. At Alexandra Palace in 1878 there were twenty-nine exhibits in the open class where Mr Hanbury's Rajah took the premier award. Entries such as those quoted were not exceptional for the mastiff, and breeders were beginning to permutate within the bloodlines which I have already outlined. Mr Hanbury retained a strong hand in mastiffs for a number of years.

The era was the most favourable for the breed. Large estates were still in vogue, communications improving, dogs shows becoming established, staff problems were non existent and the mastiff thrived. Miss Hale at Canterbury had a strong show kennel and Miss Aglionby's were rarely out of the first three places. Mr Kingdon, when not publicly denouncing the short muzzle, or dressing himself eccentrically, won a fair number of prizes with his mastiffs. In fact, he publicly stated that, since taking up the Lyme Hall dogs, he had considerably improved the strain, and would continue to do so by avoiding the Ch. King line. Another exhibitor of the period was W. K. Taunton of Hatton Garden, London, who became a world authority on the breed and retained an interest in it until his death at a great age in 1926.

As an indication of mastiff prices, Miss Aglionby bred a sensational litter containing five champions in 1867, the most famous being Ch. Turk (2349). Turk was sold to Mr T. E. Terry for four hundred and fifty pounds and later passed to Mr Robinson for five hundred and eighty pounds. Others in the litter were Ch. Wolf, King, Templar, Emperor and Prince. Argus was the same way bred but from a later litter.

Kingdon's total condemnation of Ch. King was not without some foundation but as is so often the case, by overstating his arguments he tended to have them dismissed, yet the pedigree of Ch. King is important and deserves closer study – see appendix.

King's dam Jenny was extremely short-headed, and was supposed to have been of the old Trentham strain, but was of unknown parentage. Nell 3 was a granddaughter of Lord Darnley's Nell who was undisputedly a bulldog cross. Wynn considered her to be from a 'bull mastiff dog out of a mastiff bitch' but

Kingdon maintained that the bitch was of bull terrier origin. Wynn was probably correct as his theory that Nell carried the short head would be genetically probable. Mastiff colours in the period were brindle, fawn, fallow or red, the latter colour being associated with the Lyme Hall dogs. What may be surprising to readers today is the extent which white featured on many dogs. A white blaze on the chest and running up under the chin, muzzle and over the skull had been accepted for centuries, and was not considered to be unusual. Wynn's Ch. Peeress (2393) was registered as 'light fawn, white blaze on face, white on back, and legs', whilst Mr C. Bathurst registered his Peverill (2320) as being 'mixed fawn, brindled and white'. All black mastiffs were not uncommon, in fact as recently as 1904 a mastiff of this colour was registered.

In 1873 Wynn created a furore at Birmingham by giving the first prize to the short muzzled Taurus (King ex Hanbury's Phillis), and leaving many longer muzzled champions out of the prize list. There is every possibility that when Hanbury's Prince, who carried the short-faced factor, was mated to Rowe's Nell (a litter sister to Ch. King), the short-faced factor became inbred and fixed. It was this trend, and indeed an animal of this line who brought ruin to the breed by his indiscriminate use at stud. That animal was Ch. Crown Prince.

How, or why Crown Prince became a champion is mystifying. He was yellow-eyed, dudley-nosed, lacked mask, was not straight in front, was crippled behind with completely straight stifles and no bend of hock. What he

Ch. Crown Prince. Controversy surrounded this dog, even his parentage was questioned. He had a Dudley mask and brown nose, light eyes, and extremely weak, straight and narrow hindquarters. Despite these faults, he was extensively used at stud probably because of his short head. At Dr Forbes-Winslow's auction in 1884 he was sold for 180 guineas – a high price in that era.

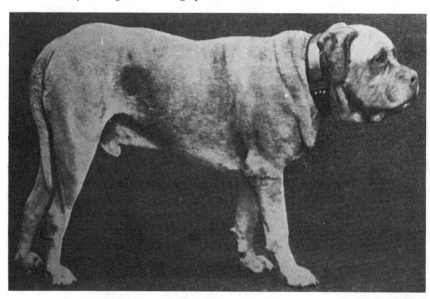

did possess was a tremendously broad, short head and square short muzzle. When his breeder, Mr Woolmore, brought him out at Alexandra Palace in 1880, many presumed that the dog would not be placed in the winning, but the judge, Rev. Mellor, not only placed him highly but bought the dog after the show. There were many criticisms and murmurings, some claiming that the pedigree of the dog was incorrect, and that he was a son of The Shah. Others considered him to have been sired by The Emperor, but an enquiry initiated by the Old English Mastiff Club could find nothing to prove that Crown Prince's pedigree was incorrect, so his official parentage remains as being by Young Prince out of Merlin. At the time when Merlin was mated, Young Prince, The Shah and The Emperor were all kennelled with Mr Burnell. The head kennelman testified that Merlin had on the instructions of Mr Burnell, been mated to The Emperor. This statement was dismissed, and so, I expect, was the kennelman.

Ch. Crown Prince had a very active stud career and passed into the owner-ship of Dr Forbes-Winslow. A decade later it was almost impossible to find a mastiff in Britain which did not go back to this very unsound dog. By coincidence his lack of mask and dudley nose were rarely passed on to his progeny, but by inbreeding to Ch. Crown Prince the mastiff was cursed with the hindquarter defects with which we are still to some extent battling. To illustrate the extent of this dog's use at stud, all but two of the fifty-one exhibits at the Old English Mastiff Club's first show at Crystal Palace on August 22 1890 were descendants of Ch. Crown Prince, many being 'blessed' with him as progenitor of both sire and dam. The dog marked a new era in the breed, and it therefore seems an appropriate place in which to temporarily leave the historical survey and assess the mastiff strain which we have already frequently mentioned – the Lyme Hall strain.

4

The Lyme Hall Mastiffs

It is not difficult to see why Wynn was unfavourably disposed towards the Lyme Hall strain, as the type was quite alien to his conception of what a mastiff should be, and to his efforts to ensure that the breed was altered to suit these ideals.

When he wrote '. . . at Lyme no record appears to have been kept of the lineage of the race, neither has any purity of type been cultivated', Wynn made invalid points. We have seen how animals which formed the basis of mastiff breeding in the early part of the nineteenth century were not only 'lacking in purity of race' but were in many instances of far more doubtful parentage than anything kept at Lyme Hall. As Lyme and its legends still feature in anything written on the breed, it is vital that we should try to get at the facts.

Lyme Hall, now National Trust Property, stands on the Lancashire/Cheshire borders near Disley and the forest of Macclesfield, an area long associated with the Legh family. My survey has been made possible through the kindness of the present head of the family, Lord Newton, whose forebears built Lyme and lived there from the sixteenth to the twentieth centuries. Lord Newton makes no special claim to knowledge of dogs in general, or mastiffs in particular, but in a letter to me he writes that as a child he would ride on the back of the last mastiffs kept at Lyme which his grandmother described as being 'as large as donkeys'.

The first recorded association of the breed and the Legh (pronounced Lee) family is contained in the story of how at the battle of Agincourt, the severely wounded Sir Piers Legh was guarded by his faithful mastiff bitch who had accompanied him to battle. The dying Sir Piers was found by English soldiers and only to these fellow countrymen would the bitch give up her precious charge. Sir Piers died in Paris from his wounds and his body was returned to England, together with the mastiff bitch, who had in the meantime given birth to pups. The Legh family have always accepted the story as fact and considered that the mastiffs who survived at Lyme from Agincourt to the 1914–18 war were her lineal descendants. Lord Newton told me that his grandfather had the last of the Lyme mastiffs destroyed during the first world war, considering it to be an act of patriotism due to the shortage of food.

Wynn points out that Henry V set sail from Southampton on 13 August 1415 and that Agincourt was fought on 25 October, i.e. sixty-three days from the date of setting sail. As the bitch was capable of being present at the battle and active enough to defend her master, Wynn felt that she must have got in whelp some time after leaving England. He further considered that in the

34

confusion, bustle and even dire straits of the English at Agincourt it is probable that no care was taken of the paternity of the litter, and therefore correct to state that the Lyme Hall race were cross-bred mongrels from the start.

The reverend gentleman was very unsporting and somewhat inconsistent in his assessment. For someone capable of accepting, and indeed inventing, theories of imports from Assyria by Phoenicians, his criticism of Lyme are unbalanced. Having dismissed the dogs as mongrels he goes on to write '. . . the mastiff being present with Sir Piers Legh at Agincourt shows that at that date the breed was often the favourite companion and guard of the wealthy'. Knights often took a favourite dog to battle with them, but this surely gives credence to the Lyme story. Instead of dismissing the progeny of the valiant Lyme bitch as being 'mongrels' Wynn should have realised that there was every possibility that other knights took their mastiffs to battle as companions. Many of us who have owned stud dogs would agree that the noise of battle, the clashings of swords and screams of horses would have meant nothing if at the time these virile males were being driven by Nature's call for procreation. Could the sire of the Lyme/Agincourt litter have been such a dog?

H. D. Kingdon was as fervently pro Lyme as Wynn was opposed to it. In the mastiff section of Webb's *Dogs, their whims, instincts and peculiarities* Kingdon allows his imagination to overide his knowledge of Lyme and its dogs. This book incidentally is a rarity nowadays but extremely useful for its plates of mastiffs of the mid-nineteenth century.

Of Sir Piers of Agincourt fame he writes, prettily, but quite inaccurately:

> . . . while wedding festivities of Sir Percy Legh were being celebrated at Lyme, a herald from his personal friend Henry V summoned him to attend His Majesty to the French wars. He at once departed leaving his bride of some weeks in grief and affliction:
>
> > To horse, to horse, Sir Percy cried,
> > Yet sought to sooth his weeping bride:
> > My trusty sword-nay, never fear-
> > My greaves, my corslet, helm, and spear

Details of the Agincourt wounding are then given, together with the return of the bitch and her pups. Kingdon proceeds to dramatise the scene:

> On reaching Macclesfield a horseman was despatched to announce to Lady Agnes Legh the approach of her husband's body and funeral cortège. This messenger met her in the park on a high point now marked with a belvedere called Lyme Cage. Her reason fled, never to return, she became a wandering maniac and was ultimately found dead on her husband's grave.

This is absolute fiction. Sir Piers Legh married at the age of thirteen, a custom usual in feudal times, his wife being Joan, daughter and heiress to Sir Gilbert de Haydock. Far from losing her wits as Kingdon stated, the widow remarried, her second husband being Sir Richard Molyneaux, another knight of Agincourt. It was a prolific union, as eight sons and three daughters were born to them.

One must view all Kingdon's writings with a high degree of scepticism. He was a breed enthusiast, eccentric and colourful, but his imagination equalled his love of the breed.

As Wynn and others had such serious doubts of the existence of any mastiffs at Lyme, I have gone to some length to prove such existence. It was a time-consuming but worthwhile project, and one admits that the fortunes and misfortunes of the family itself became far more interesting than the search for mastiffs. The one way in which one can prove mastiff existence is by checking family records and making notes of any references. The muniments of the family were made available to me, and from the seventeenth century onwards the breed is mentioned as such. Prior to this there are references to dogs but not specifically mastiffs, though these too could have been mastiffs.

In the house accounts for 1612 we find 'for stufe to dress mastiv, 6d'. I wonder what trouble the mastiff had to need such expenditure.

In 1612 Anne Legh (great-granddaughter of the Agincourt Sir Piers) married Richard Bold of Bold, a wealthy Lancashire squire. The marriage took place at Lyme, and the parish register of Farmworth Church confirms this. The family connection between Legh and Bold seems to have escaped the attention of Wynn and others, but Wynn admired the Bold strain. What would have been more probable than for Anne to have taken a favourite dog when leaving her much loved home. To perpetuate the line would it not have been logical for her to have returned to the home strain? Anne was a regular visitor to Lyme as the letters proved.

Wynn writes of a dog as being 'One of the noted strain of English mastiffs from the fine old residence of Bold Hall'. He also quotes a letter from Col. Wilson Patten '. . . the Bold mastiff is a light tawny colour, that of Lyme is much darker, almost amounting to red. The former has a light, and the latter a black muzzle. In these later years there have been crosses between the two to the advantage of both.'

I have an interesting letter to Sir Piers Legh dated 1615*. It was written by Sir John Egerton, a nephew who later became the first Lord Bridgwater. In a wonderfully bold hand with all the lettering embellishments common at the time he wrote as a postcript to his uncle 'You have long known me as a "swift dog dealer", but not for a mastiff monger. Yet I must earnestly pray you that by your means, and my Aunts, I may have a good brave dog. I pray you let me be holding to you for such a one or more, for when I can get him I would either get a good one or none.' The English has been brought up to date for easier reading but was Sir John punning on the words 'swift dog dealer'? If he was, the mastiff was slower, and probably heavy.

Sir Piers Legh was obviously sympathetic to his nephew's request, as a further letter in the same year reads:

> . . . I have been uncommonly lucky in begging those mastiffs from my aunt and your good self, which you sent up with Mr Eastley. My wife requires me to send

---

* Piers was very much a family name with the result that there is a confusing succession of heads of the family bearing the name.

her kind thanks for the dogs, and her loving remembrances to my aunt and your self.

Your very loving and respectful nephew

Egerton.

Earlier mention of Lyme and the dogs will be found in Stowe's *Annals* where a pair were among the gifts sent in 1604 by James I to Philip of Spain. The presents accompanied the Oath of the Confirmation of the Articles of Peace at the close of England's war with Spain. The section of interest to us is 'a cupple of Lyme hounds of singular qualities'. Lady Newton in her *House of Lyme* felt that these were mastiffs as '. . . in the great picture by Velaquez of the children of Philip IV, "Las Meninas", which hangs in Madrid, a large mastiff is seen in the foreground one of the children rubbing its back with his foot. The dog is precisely the same as the Lyme mastiffs of the present day, having all their characteristics and was, no doubt, a descendant of the pair presented by James I to Philip III in 1604'. Could these dogs have been the progenitors of the present day Mastin Espagnol?

The Egerton letters quoted above prove that there were mastiffs at Lyme in the early seventeenth century making Lady Newton's theory possible. In all fairness to Lady Newton's opinions, one must realise that her assessments, written in 1917, were those of an interested observer, and not the specialist appraisal of a dog judge. Lady Newton described the Lyme Hall mastiffs as '. . . now alas threatened with extinction. The breed has existed at Lyme for generations; the dogs are noted for their immense size, being almost as large as donkeys. They are pale lemon in colour, with gigantic heads somewhat resembling bloodhounds, black ears and muzzles, immensely broad chests, and soft brown eyes.' Robert Dudley, the great favourite of Elizabeth I who was created Earl of Leicester also had a mastiff from Lyme Hall. In a letter addressed to 'My very loving friend Sir Piers Legh, Knight' he thanks Sir Piers for allowing him to have the dog and 'will requyte you the loss of him with as good a thinge'.

The baronetcy of Newton was granted in 1872, and it is of some significance that the first Lord Newton chose, as supporters to the coat of arms 'two mastiffs proper collared sable'. One accepts that the animals portrayed in the crest were probably not current Lyme types, but the first Baron obviously wished to perpetuate the breed's association with his family. In the Royal Academy exhibition of 1908 there was a portrait of Lord Newton with a mastiff at his side, and the breed is also depicted in a stained glass window at Lyme Hall.

The present Lord Newton, in a letter to me on the subject, says: 'It may be – I do not know – that at some point in the nineteenth century the original strain died out at Lyme, and the breed was reintroduced'. Wynn expressed the gravest doubts of the existence of the true mastiff at Lyme, and J. W. Thompson, the pioneer breeder whom we have already discussed, is alleged to have sent an agent there to inspect the dogs. Thompson's report was that such dogs that were at the old residence were the true boarhound type, and were red in colour. At a later date (25 March 1873) he wrote that the Lyme Hall mastiffs were 'a myth'.

From an engraving in the author's collection. 'Beth – Lyme Hall' is written on the back of the engraving. Circa 1890.

Against this we have the opinion of H. D. Kingdon writing about the same time: 'I now breed from the original kennels with the consent of Mr Legh and I have, at this time, a stud equal to, if not surpassing, the Lyme breed.' Modesty was not one of Mr Kingdon's more obvious qualities. He continues: '. . . in some circles it was rumoured that the old Lyme strain had become almost extinct but that Mr Legh had other mastiff types present which were being crossed with the original strain'. This other strain to which rumour referred were (in Mr Legh's words) 'Lord Stamford's breed of night dogs used by the keepers'. This would suggest that they were bull mastiffs, and I wonder whether Lord Newton's letter, in which he queries if a strain was reintroduced in the nineteenth century, refers to these crossings which resuscitated Lyme mastiffs. Kingdon maintains that he discussed the possibility of crossings with Mr Legh, and was informed that no crossings had taken place. For all his odd opinions, I liked his assessment of the breed, written nearly a century ago, as it has an all too familiar echo in the present day.

> The fancy breed now in vogue is much too cut up in flank, is not massive enough, and is deficient in bone. The mastiff pure is more thickset with a barrel nearly straight underneath, and with shorter and larger legs, bone being of consequence in the mastiff proper. We do not believe the purity of mastiffs over thirty inches.

From the evidence which I have quoted, it is obvious that there were mastiffs at Lyme over many generations, and we have already seen that mastiffs of the famous strain were used in the recorded mastiff breeding in the mid nineteenth century. What we have been unable to prove is the value of Lyme animals as show specimens of the breed, as so few pictures exist. George Earl, the well known dog portrait painter was fascinated by Kingdon's 'Barry', a pure Lyme Hall dog, and painted him on more than one occasion. One of these paintings is now in the offices of the American Kennel Club. Kingdon was deeply attached to Barry and refused a three hundred guinea offer for him in 1870.

What probably happened at Lyme was that as the result of long inbreeding to animals carrying undesirable factors, the strain began to degenerate. Rawdon Lee in 1894 summarised the position:

> . . . I do not think that anyone who wishes to improve his strain of mastiffs today would fly to Lyme Hall kennels for the purpose. At the time of my visit there was a fine painting by Nettleship about 1876 of a mastiff and a right good one too (evidently quite as good as Miss Aglionby's Turk) and some others that have had more to do with the foundation of our present strain than some people imagine.

As a final note on Lyme Hall, I should mention that the Lyme Hall used as an affix on some post-war American pedigrees is in no way connected with the old English residence, except that for all of us Lyme Hall mastiffs are the ancestors of today's dogs.

5

Mastiffs from Late Nineteenth Century to 1914 War

The decade which preceeded the advent of Ch. Crown Prince was a period of mastiff popularity, which the breed was never able to regain. Dog shows were comparatively new, and the support given to such shows by mastiff exhibitors was unequalled. Instances of such support show not only the level of enthusiasm, but the numerical strength of the breed at this time. Compared with present day figures, top competition must have been particularly strong. At the New Agricultural Hall Islington in 1862, there were thirty-nine exhibits in one class, and in 1870 the mastiff entry at Crystal Palace was the largest in the non-sporting group, a feat repeated in Birmingham in 1872. The mastiff entry was the highest per class of any breed scheduled at the Crystal Palace in 1876 and at the Kennel Club's Show 1878 Mr Hanbury's Rajah won the open class competing against twenty-nine exhibits. Such notable persons as HRH The Prince of Wales (later King Edward VII) was a mastiff owner, and the breed was a great favourite of Lord Byron.

Why then the decline? Some suggest that it was due to the unsoundness which Ch. Crown Prince transmitted to his progeny, making mastiff breeding a hazardous affair. Others at the time suggested that the fashionable short head had robbed the mastiff of the dignity and outline which owners expected of the breed, but the true answer remains unsolved. Ch. Crown Prince did beget crippled mastiffs, and short-headed types. Perhaps breeders should have paid more attention to the deteriorating movement, but obviously the rot had set in.

A mastiff club was formed in 1873 mainly through the efforts of Rev. Wynn, who became its first secretary. It was probably Wynn who introduced the rule which caused the club's early demise, when insisting under threat of expulsion that members could exhibit their mastiffs only at shows where the officiating judge was a member of the club. One cannot but suspect that Wynn hoped to indoctrinate such judges with the necessity of giving high awards to short-headed mastiffs only, thus effecting the change which he had long advocated. Ten years later the Old English Mastiff Club was formed, and remains one of the oldest breed clubs in Britain today. In the interwar period there were two other registered mastiff clubs, The Northern Mastiff Club, and the Mastiff Breeders Association, but both were defunct by 1939.

In 1984 the author called an open meeting at Highnam Court, Gloucestershire, with the proposal of forming a new mastiff club. As the result of this meeting the Mastiff Association was formed and accepted by The Kennel Club as a registered breed club in 1986.

Founders of the Old English Mastiff Club included Rev. Mellor, Dr Forbes-

Winslow and Mr W. K. Taunton. It was this body that drew up the breed standard in the form which is almost identical to the one used by the Kennel Club today. There have been a few revisions and rewordings, but it is remarkably similar. Dr Forbes-Winslow owned a very fashionable house at 23 Cavendish Square, in London's West End. His kennels were dispersed in December 1883 when Ch. Crown Prince was auctioned for one hundred and eighty guineas. Other mastiffs of his realised some very modest prices.

Another pioneer, Dr Sidney Turner had a distinguished career in medicine, being an authority on obstetrics and becoming Chairman of the newly formed Kennel Club. He discontinued direct breeding of mastiffs after the second generation, but remained as a judge of the breed for many years. Among the animals which he bred was Ch. Orlando and Ch. Hotspur, Ch. Lady Isabel, the latter bitch the dam of the outstanding Ch. Beaufort, acknowledged to be the best mastiff at the turn of the century. Although Beaufort carried the Ch. Crown Prince line (his dam was a Crown Prince daughter) the unsoundness of hindquarters were not transmitted to him; he probably followed his sire, Ch. Beau in this respect. Both Ch. Orlando and Ch. Hotspur were grand-headed mastiffs, but both were questionable in hindquarters. It was probably this which prompted Dr Turner not to use these dogs extensively at stud, although for head qualities they must have been unsurpassed. There are at least six recorded litters sired by Hotspur and three by Orlando. Some of the matings occurred after the dogs had left the immediate control of their owner. Both dogs, although apparently passed to other hands, remained in the legal ownership of Dr Turner. He probably intended to take up mastiff breeding again, and could have picked up the strain had he so wished. W. K. Taunton took over Ch. Hotspur and in a letter which was part of a small collection of Mr Taunton's papers in the possession of the late Mrs Scheerboom, explained the ownership of both dogs to Mr Hawkings (Snr). Mrs Anne Davies of Nantymynydd has a fine old collar which was worn by one of Dr Turner's dogs and it may be of some significance that the collar will not comfortably fit the necks of some of Mrs Davies's present dogs. This would suggest that Dr Turner's dogs were not as large as some would have us believe.

Mr W. K. Taunton, who purchased Ch. Beaufort, sent the dog to the USA for a while when the partnership of Taunton, in England and Winchell, Vermont USA was in being. This was, of course, prior to quarantine regulations in Britain. It was a unique example of trans Atlantic co-operation. It was probably this partnership which suggested that The Old English Mastiff Club should organise an American Branch and Committee. The venture did not prove to be satisfactory and was disbanded at a Club special meeting in 1889.

A dog who should have remained in Britain, where he would have been invaluable as an outcross to the Crown Prince line, was Ch. Minting, bred by Mrs Willins by Maximilian (grandson of Rajah) out of Ch. Cambrian Princess. Minting had an excellent head, good hind angulation and powerful forehand; in fact apart from a slack topline, which was a fault in many mastiffs of the period Minting would be a pace setter today. He was exported in 1888 and had died before Ch. Beaufort arrived in the USA. It would have been interesting to see how these two great dogs would have compared in the show circuits.

Mr R. Cook of Cranbrook Lodge, Ilford, Essex became the Old English Mastiff Club's first secretary, having already established his mastiff kennel, and adopted the now common practice of registering stock with an individual prefix, in his case 'Ilford'. Ilford Cromwell (born 1881) and bred by W. K. Taunton was exported to the USA as were Ilford Cambria, and Ilford Chancellor. Mr Moore, a USA breed enthusiast, paid two hundred pounds for the latter dog, who became a pillar of the breed in America. Ilford Cromwell, incidentally, was a blue brindle, a colour unacceptable today but not unknown in mastiffs. Cromwell was from a fawn brindle to fawn brindle mating, but could possibly have reverted to their common ancestor, Mr Lukey's Bruce 2, who was a blue brindle.

Capt Piddocke of Ross-on-Wye, Herefordshire was a well known breeder and much sought after judge of mastiffs of the era. Mr Mark Beaufoy who owned Ch. Beau was active as a breeder of sound mastiffs, but the longer skulls of his strain did not find favour in the new vogue for the shorter head. Rev. Mellor somehow managed to judge the breed all over the country, in addition to his parochial duties in Cheltenham.

By 1890 registrations had fallen to one hundred and sixteen and ten years later only twenty-four were registered during the year. But throughout the chequered history of the mastiff there seems always to have been a nucleus of stalwarts prepared to carry on the difficult task of preserving the breed, and such a nucleus at the turn of the century managed to turn the tide in the breed's favour. Mr R. Leadbetter of Hazelmere, Bucks, was one such person who forsook his winning Great Danes for the mastiff cause. Leadbetter was a colourful character, a Master of Foxhounds, and an admirer of bears; in fact he kept a few of these at his house. He died in comparative poverty, unrecognisably unkempt, and greatly reduced in circumstances; but this cannot be totally attributed to the mastiff, though there is a strong tradition that the mastiff either breaks your heart, or your finances.

Leadbetter's kennels often housed forty or more mastiffs, and at one time Hazlemere could boast eight champions present, all under the age of four. The brindled champions Marksman and Marcella were fine specimens of the breed, Marcella being strong-boned, and broad-chested. Perhaps she would have been somewhat short on the leg for some present day tastes, but what weight and power this bitch must have possessed! The short-headed type was very much a Leadbetter requirement; in fact his Prince Sonderberg (born 1903) had so short a muzzle as to be confused with that of a modern bullmastiff. In Mr Leadbetter's own words, the long muzzle was 'an abomination', but it wasn't only on heads that he had definite views. He defined his ideal body type as being 'built like a little carthorse, and on cloddy lines'. His most famous mastiff was undoubtedly Ch. Elgiva who was much publicised photographically, and painted by J. D. Redworth. Redworth's painting appears in Cassell's *New Book of the Dog*. Elgiva was certainly short faced and possessed hind dewclaws which had not been removed. It isn't often that mastiff puppies are born with these nowadays, but some years ago I bred a bullmastiff litter in which three puppies had hind dewclaws.

An interesting, if rather elusive figure in the breed from 1875 until his death in 1931 was Col. Zaccheus Walker of Fox Hollies Hall, near Birmingham. Col. Walker was not an enthusiastic exhibitor, but the soundness of his Ch. Britain's Belle and Britain's Queen could not be overlooked. In a show report on Britain's Queen it is recorded that she moved with a freedom and precision that would be hard to beat in any breed. Col. Walker probably realised the necessity of getting away from the orthodox bloodlines to achieve good movement, as Britain's Belle's bloodlines contain several of unknown origin.

In 1913 sixty mastiffs were registered and at the outbreak of the First World War the numerical strength of the breed still left much to be desired.

The survey of mastiffs of the period is concluded with two charts of precise measurements and weights of well known dogs. Dr Sidney Turner, Chairman of the Kennel Club, published the charts in an article on the breed in his *The Kennel Encyclopaedia* of 1910. Note that the winners were animals of good weight and substance but were not tall dogs. Ch. Beaufort was considered by many to have been the ideal size, and type for a mastiff.

It may be interesting to give the monthly rate of increase in weight of a few celebrated Mastiff dogs and bitches.

Months....	*1*	*2*	*3*	*4*	*5*	*6*	*7*	*8*	*9*	*10*	*11*	*12*
Orlando ....lbs....	10–13	23½	43	69	88	110	124	140	148	154	160	170
Hotspur ....lbs....	8½	15	35	51	70	89	98	110	114	115	121	130
The Lady Gladys ...lbs....	8–11	16–4	37	58	68	83	92½	107	115	118	115½	120
The Lady Isabel.....lbs....	9– 3	17–4	40	58	70	92	97½	110	114	120	118½	120

It may also be well to give the weights of a few at full growth, with other particulars.

	Height at Shoulder in.	*Weight lbs*	*Girth of Chest in.*	*Girth of Skull in.*	*Girth of Muzzle in.*	*Girth of Forearm in.*	*Length of Skull in.*	*Length of Muzzle in.*	*Length from Nose to Occiput in.*	*From Nose to Rest of Tail in.*	*Length of Tail in.*
Beaufort	29½	165	42	27	16½	12	7½	4	11½	52½	19½
Jack Thyr	28½	156	38½	27	16	11¼	7	3½	10½	49½	20
Wodan	30	160	41	26½	16¼	11½	7½	3½	11	51½	24
Orlando	29	172	44	29½	17½	12½	8	4	12	50	21
Hotspur	28	132	38	27	16½	11	8	4	12	49	19
The Lady Gladys......	26	128	36	24½	15	10½	7	3	10	49	17
The Lady Isabel.......	27	135	36	23	14½	10	6½	3½	10	51	18

6

From 1918 to Present Day

When peace was declared in 1918 the breed had numerically weakened. Social changes and the breaking up of country estates had not helped the mastiff, yet indirectly the scarcity of stock proved to be its salvation as outcrosses, chiefly with unregistered mastiffs or mastiff types, were resorted to and once again the mastiff was resuscitated.

Animals suitable for outcrossing were not too difficult to find as many gamekeepers owned dogs which contained more mastiff than anything else, and whilst purists shook their heads and felt that crosses would ruin the breed, not only did the mastiff survive, and breed true, it in many ways showed an improvement in soundness. I am an advocate of inbreeding where no hereditary weakness exists, but where such factors are present, and the bloodlines close, or limited, the only long term solution to the problem is to outcross. Col. Z. Walker demonstrated this in his Ch. Britain's Queen and Belle, and the two important stud dogs which we shall next consider both carried the same bitch as an outcross, yet these two dogs sired many good mastiffs in the inter-war period. Both were bred by George Cook, who took over his father's 'Cleveland' prefix.

The first dog which we will look at briefly was Ch. Felix, born 1906 but still alive in 1918; the other, Ch. Brompton Duke, born in 1910, also survived into the inter-war years. Ch. Felix was by Nuneaton Lion out of a brindled bitch called Kitty Marton. Ch. Brompton Duke was by Cleveland Leopold out of Felicia, a daughter of Kitty Marton. All that we know of Kitty Marton was that she was out of an unregistered brindled bitch called Floss. Floss was acquired by George Cook but with no knowledge of her breeding, or background. She may have been a pure mastiff, but whatever she was, she was sound, and both mastiffs and bullmastiffs trace back to her.

It was chiefly George Cook's Cleveland Kennels which supplied the foundation stock of Mr Bennett's Broomcourt Kennels at Rotherham, a leading establishment until the outbreak of the second war, specialising in brindles of good solid type. Mr Bennett's advertisements of the early 1930s were original, and typical: 'We aim to fill England with mastiffs of type and quality to beat the elephant and giraffe monstrosities'. Another of his advertisements runs 'Type before tonnage – down the centuries the mastiff has been the supreme defender of the nobility. He evolved broad, square, deep, massive jaws in order to get a grip on his natural foe. It is therefore obvious that misnamed mastiffs with muzzles like sheepdogs are mongrels'. Forty years later, one still sees truth in what Mr Bennett wrote, as even today there are persons who insist

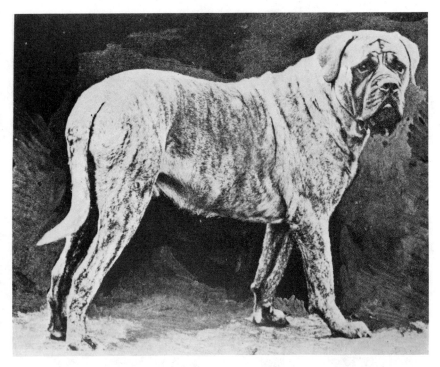

Ch. Felix (born 1906) by Nuneaton Lion ex Kitty Marton (unregistered). This dog could easily win in the show-ring today.

on looking at height as being indicative of size and will applaud the elephantine of indifferent quality.

To return to Ch. Brompton Duke. He was used at stud by R. J. Burch of Ponders End, Middlesex. Mr Burch was a dairyman and keen mastiff exhibitor who at that time owned a very sound bitch called Galazora. Mated to Ch. Brompton Duke, two mastiffs of importance were produced, John Bull and Young Mary Bull who later became a champion. These two (full brother and sister) were in due course mated together and produced two champions Ch. King Baldur and Ch. The Scarlet Pimpernel.

Ch. King Baldur had several owners, but did the major part of his stud work and ended his days in the ownership of R. J. W. Conquest, who had established a small but select kennels at The Bannut Tree, Castlemorton, near Malvern. Mr Conquest was a Master of Foxhounds and a keen sportsman, but after a generation or so of mastiff breeding he gave it up, retaining the dogs as companions. Ch. King Baldur is of great importance to this historical survey, not only for his importance as a mastiff sire, but because he represents one of the first stages of the emergence of the bullmastiff as a pure breed.

Another important figure of the 1920s was Mr Guy Greenwood who owned many good mastiffs including the tall reddish Ch. Duke. Guy Greenwood's father James had been a mastiff owner and breeder, and the family connections

45

passed to Guy's daughter Dorothy who became the third generation of the family to be associated with the breed. After her marriage, there was no active participation in the breed, but her recent donation of a scrapbook showing many of the old mastiffs and their pedigrees, has been greatly appreciated by the Old English Mastiff Club who were the fortunate recipients.

Miss I. Bell, an important figure in the breed both before and after the Second World War, bred her first mastiff litter in 1924. Her interest in mastiffs went back to childhood days, when taken by her parents to Crufts show. She apparently saw a mastiff there, standing on its hind legs with its paws round its owner's neck, which made her determined to own one of these dogs when she grew up. Miss Bell's first dogs were from Mr Burch's strain out of a Westrcroft bitch. The Westcroft Kennels, owned by Mrs Kennett, were at Lower Earley,

Broomcourt in 1938. Miss Mary Bennett with (left to right) Broomcourt Etta, Broomcourt Jem and Ch. Comedienne of Broomcourt.

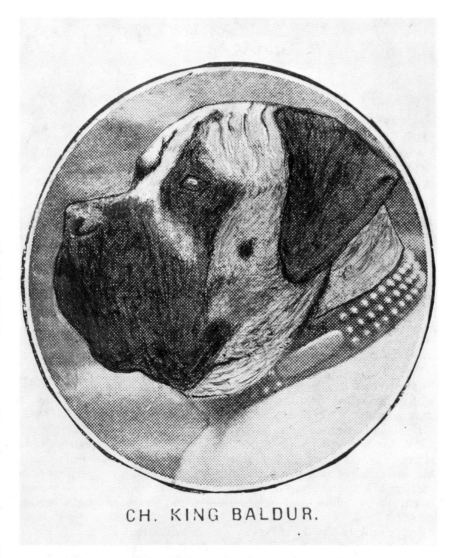

CH. KING BALDUR.

Ch. King Baldur. An important sire in the evolution of the bullmastiff. See pedigree of Ch. Roger of the Fenns in Appendix.

Ch. Young Mary Bull. This bitch features in the pedigrees of both mastiffs and bullmastiffs (see pedigree of Ch. Roger of the Fenns in appendix).

Reading, and disbanded in 1924. Miss Bell bred Ch. Woden in this litter, a dog who in due course sired three champions for Miss Bell in his first litter. A great-grandson of Ch. Woden in the early 1930s was Ch. Uther Penarvon, a very strong headed, and heavily built fawn. The kennels were originally near Ascot, but later moved to Great Withybush, Cranleigh, Surrey: hence the prefix 'Withybush' which was registered after the war. Miss Bell's contribution to the post-war mastiff is dealt with later in this chapter, but some measure of her success can be gauged from the fact that she bred six pre-war champions as well as many other prize winners, most of which she handled herself.

In the early 1920s Mr and Mrs F. Scheerboom entered the mastiff scene. It is a great pleasure to be able to record some of the contributions which their Havengore kennels made to the mastiffs and to pay tribute to Mrs L. Scheerboom, undoubtedly the world's greatest authority on the breed, who despite her eighty odd years remained as interested in mastiffs up to the time of her death as she was half a century earlier when she and her husband purchased their first bitch, Crescent Rowena.

Mrs Scheerboom once told me of her childhood ambition to own a bulldog. Although much favoured by an indulgent grandfather, the line was drawn at what he called 'snuffling bulldogs' and so the much craved ownership of this breed did not materialise until after her marriage. As a result of their activities in the dog world Mr and Mrs Scheerboom met Sam Woodiwiss, who had owned mastiffs but whose main interest at that time lay in bulldogs and Siamese cats, then a novelty in Britain. Mrs Scheerboom also developed an interest in Siamese and owned at least one pair of them for a number of years.

Their first mastiff purchase, a bitch called Crescent Rowena was by Duke of Ashenhurst out of Shirebrook Lady. Shirebrook Lady was by Ch. King Baldur out of Penkhull Lady, a bullmastiff cross. Penkhull Lady was by the bull-mastiff Stapleford Agrippa out of Helen, who was presumed to be a mastiff but was of unknown parentage, and unregistered.

The first mastiff litter was born in 1925. Crescent Rowena had been mated to Miss Harbur's Ch. Master Beowulf whose pedigree was incomplete, and who was not placed at public stud. From this litter came Ch. Bill of Havengore large, sound, fawn and who grew on to be a truly great mastiff. His brother Jack of Havengore left his mark. The Havengore mastiffs were used at stud by discriminating breeders, to the distinct improvement of the mastiff, especially in head type and expression.

The Havengores were strong in bitches, and there were as many as ten or so in the kennels, all broad, well-boned, big-ribbed animals of the type associated with the prefix.

The post war achievements are dealt with later, but one should record that

Miss B. Blackstone handling a quartet of Miss I. Bell's mastiffs in early 1920s. Left to right: Ch. Cleopatra of Westcroft, Helga, Woden and Lady Hildur.

49

the success of the Havengores was based on the refusal to accept the second rate. During the fifty years of the kennel's existence, there was never any commercialism, neither was there ever what has now become the accepted practice of rearing every puppy born. The stock was always culled, as Mrs Scheerboom had an intimate knowledge of the bloodlines with which she was dealing, and realised that only by the elimination of genetically associated faults could type upgrading be achieved. Against this I should add that Mrs Scheerboom knew each of her dogs as personalities within their own rights and the idiosyncracies of many of the early dogs were clearly remembered. Crescent Rowena (pet named 'Trixie') was remembered for the quality of companionship which she gave to her owners, and her devotion to the household's favourite Siamese cat. When the cat died of cat 'flu, Trixie mourned the death for weeks as the cat was her constant companion and bedmate. Trixie may have carried a bullmastiff cross, but there are few good mastiffs today who do not go back to her chiefly through Ch. Bill of Havengore.

Another important kennel was that of Mrs Edger, whose Deleval prefix was often in the awards. Two which spring to mind were Torfreda of Deleval, an exceptionally sound bitch, and Sir Galahad of Deleval who in his prime tipped

'Crescent Rowena'. The foundation of the Havengore Kennel. See pedigree in Appendix.

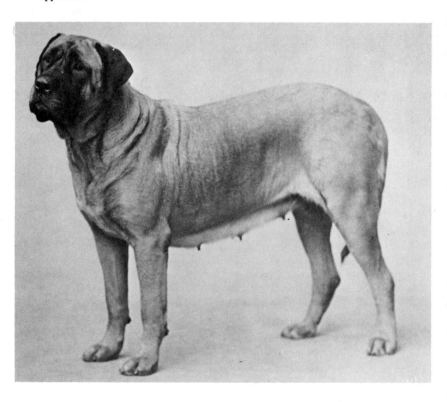

The first Havengore litter born in 1925. Sire: Ch. Master Beowulf. Dam: Crescent Rowena.

Mrs L. Scheerboom with some of her mastiffs. Ch. Hotspot of Havengore in background. Left to right: Adam of Havengore; Nectar of Havengore; Caradog of Havengore.

the scales at sixteen stone and was considered to be the largest mastiff in Britain. Mrs Edger fed her mastiffs a good deal of goat's milk and was a firm believer in its abilities to promote growth. Deleval bloodlines went back to Ashenhurst, Cleveland, and Havengore, via Ch. Bill.

At the same time Mr H. Taylor's Saxondale kennels were active and the Misses Harrison owned a few mastiffs. Miss M. Harrison retains an interest in the breed and occasionally judges it.

Another flourishing kennel was that of Mr F. J. Hawkings whose notes in *Our Dogs* were featured for many years, and whose Goldhawk mastiffs were well known. It was with Mr Hawkings that Mr W. K. Taunton spent the last years of his long life, and Mr Hawkings therefore had the benefit of Mr Taunton's vast experience. Mr Hawkings was an accomplished sculptor and at the time of his death there were one or two fine mastiff head studies and a few couchant mastiff figures. There was also a collection of Mr Taunton's letters and notes which apparently went to the USA with the exception of those which Mrs Scheerboom managed to acquire.

Mrs N. Dicken developed her Goring kennels in the late 1920s, keeping mastiffs and border terriers. She became Secretary of the Old English Mastiff Club in 1932 and it is her post-war work for the breed which will always keep her name alive. In 1935 she was co-author of a book on the Mastiff and St Bernard which was to be published by Watmoughs. At the time of publication,

The world-famous cellist Beatrice Harrison with a group of mastiffs owned by Beatrice and her two sisters in the inter-war period. Miss Margaret Harrison still judges the breed and was appointed to judge mastiffs at Leicester Championship Show, 1987.

Mrs Dicken with a team of her mastiffs in 1926.

Miss I. Bell's Brockwell of Loring. Broomcourt Faithful with their 3-month-old puppy, 'Brennus'.

Broomcourt Difiant and Broomcourt Faithfull owned by Miss I. Bell.

Mr E. G. Oliver brought an action in Chancery, restraining Mrs Dicken from publishing the book as it contained articles over which he claimed copyright. Mr Oliver's action succeeded and the book was withdrawn by the publishers. Mr Oliver was awarded twenty shillings damages against Mrs Dicken but the very considerable court costs were awarded against her. Having seen a copy of the book, I cannot understand how one could claim copyright on articles which represent little else but common knowledge. The publication is so innocuous that it could hardly have caused offence, and I think that Mrs Dicken must have been very unfortunate in the whole affair.

As an interesting aside, prices for mastiffs in the 1930s were comparatively low. Puppies were advertised in the weekly journals for as little as two guineas at eight weeks, and even at six months, a promising puppy was sold for a mere seven pounds. Stud fees were comparatively high, a factor which nowadays seems to have been practically reversed. At one time the stud fee was approximately the cost of a puppy, but with present day high puppy prices, I cannot think that this principle is still applicable. In 1926 Mr J. Illingworth was charging a stud fee of eight guineas for Ch. Cedric of Ashenhurst, and this was considered to be one of the highest stud fees for any mastiff in Britain. There were some interesting articles offered for barter for mastiff puppies. One offered a six month old puppy in exchange for a full sized billiards table. Another offered 'an old violin' as exchange for an adult mastiff.

Mr Illingworth contributed to *Our Dogs* weekly mastiff notes post-war and

Mrs N. Dicken. Secretary of the Old English Mastiff Club, 1932–1964.

Mr and Mrs E. G. Oliver with a Hellingly team in the 1920s.
Left to right: Joseph of Hellingly; Hecuba of Hellingly; Boadicea of Hellingly;
Ch. Joy of Wantley; Lumbering Sheila; Lady Here of Hellingly; Almost of
Hellingly; Flavia of Westcroft.

was one of the early judges when the breed was revived in Britain. His Ch. Cedric of Ashenhurst was out of Ch. Boadicea, a daughter of Ch. The Scarlet Pimpernel, thus going back to Ch. Brompton Duke and helps to demonstrate what an exceptional force Brompton Duke was in the breed. Ch. Cedric of Ashenhurst was not quite perfect in front, but had the overall size and sound temperament to make him an attractive stud proposition. He was another of those studs who sired three champions in one litter. Mr Illingworth owned an exceptionally good one in Ch. Broomcourt Marcon, an attractive brindle.

A successful inter-war period partnership in mastiffs was that of C. R. Oliver, who kept The Hydro at Buxton, and his friend R. H. Thomas who had previously resided in the USA. R. H. Thomas was a colourful character; a Welshman by birth, he emigrated to America and for a while worked as a rodeo rider. From this he graduated to Hollywood and featured in films in which he could utilise his considerable abilities as a horseman. *The Four Horsemen of the Apocalypse* saw him in the star role. He later became entertainments manager of an exclusive Yosemite Valley hotel before returning to Britain and setting up partnership at Buxton. Parties given for mastiff enthusiasts at The Hydro were occasions which few missed; in fact The Hydro became a mecca for breed enthusiasts. There were not many mastiffs in the establishment but Ch. Yosemite Menai features in some of the old Havengore pedigrees through her son Mark of Havengore who was by Ch. Bill of Havengore. Ch.

Yosemite Menai was by Ch. King Baldur out of Bernice of Ashenhurst, a daughter of Ch. Boadicea. Thus she represents the successful Ch. Brompton Duke line, as Ch. King Baldur was strongly inbred to Brompton Duke, and Ch. Boadicea carried the Brompton Duke line as well.

Two names normally associated with bullmastiffs were mastiff owners at this time. Vic Smith, later to become a household name in bullmastiffs, purchased the mastiff King Agrippa in 1934 paying thirty-five pounds for him, this being one of the first of the breed which he owned. It is not so widely known that Vic Smith also owned a mastiff bitch post-war, and would have bred from her had she been fertile at that time. The fact that where Vic and others failed another succeeded is part of the post-war story. Mr S. E. Moseley of Burslem, Stoke on Trent was another bullmastiff pioneer who owned, and bred mastiffs at this time, but whose mastiff influence was comparatively small. There were other kennels such as those of Miss Hutchings, who owned one or two good ones.

In this necessarily condensed account, it is impossible to review all kennels, but we must end with a brief account of what was probably the most important kennel, that of Mrs E. G. Oliver at Hellingly, Winkenhurst, Sussex. Mr E. G. Oliver was partner in a practice of London solicitors and possessed that rare combination of breeder, author and student of his chosen breed. His first acquisitions on which to found his wife's kennel were Joseph of Studland and Joy of Wantley. Joseph was re-registered as Joseph of Hellingly and became a champion, as did his kennel companion.

Mr Oliver's researches into the breed brought him to the conclusion that the short foreface was foreign to the mastiff and had been brought about by bulldog crosses. He therefore set his sights on a longer-muzzled, taller animal, this being what he considered to be closer to the true mastiff. There were criticisms of his opinion, but as we have seen in earlier chapters Oliver's observations were not without a basis of historical truth. What was more factual, and a point which he chose not to recognise, was that there had always been such a variety of shapes and forms in the breed that his opinion was no further (or nearer) the truth than those advocating the short foreface. Mrs Oliver decided that size in the mastiff could only be achieved if an almost completely meat diet was fed supplemented by goats milk. A small herd of goats was installed at Hellingly for this purpose.

Much of the breed information compiled by Mr Oliver was as the result of his researches at the British Museum into the old canine literature. One of his important contributions was the writing of the mastiff section of *Hutchinson's Dog Encyclopaedia* which was published in 1935. There is one error in the text re Ch. Orlando and Ch. Hotspur, but the book also has a photographic error which may not have been the fault of the author. A photograph of the fine bitch Ch. Boadicea is printed above a caption and criticism of the dog Poor Joe. Many have been puzzled by the caption, as Ch. Boadicea was one of the soundest and best, whereas Poor Joe was decidely bow-legged in front, a fault which he seemed not to pass on.

The Olivers' ascent in the world of dogs can only be described as meteoric. Mr Oliver became a member of the Kennel Club Committee and one of the founders of the Big Breeds Association in 1932. He founded the Mastiff

Mrs E. G. Oliver with (left to right) Ch. Joseph of Hellingly (six CCs, Hannibal of Hellingly; Ch. Joy of Wantley (Hannibal's grandmother).

Breeders Association in 1930 with Viscount Weymouth as its first President. The strength and prestige of this break-away organisation can be judged by the fact that its membership boasted such well known canine elite as J. V. Rank, the Duchess of Newcastle, Mrs Vlasto and Sir John Buchanan Jardine who became its second President. If Mr Oliver was the public relations officer and breed student, Mrs Oliver specialised in rearing, feeding, and showing the many mastiffs soon built up at Hellingly. There was of course, kennel staff as well as house staff and as Mrs Phyllis Robson, *Dog World's* roving reporter once said of the mastiff entry at Harrogate 'Mrs Oliver entered twenty-nine mastiffs and brought along twenty-one which represents over a ton of mastiff'.

One of the achievements of Hellingly was the fight to re-establish the brindle colour, and when one considers that until Mrs Oliver made up her Ch. Marksman of Hellingly in 1934, there had not been a brindle champion dog since Ch. Viscount of Lidgett in 1913, this was no mean achievement. Mrs Oliver was elected to the committee of the Scottish Kennel Club and became a mastiff specialist judge of the pre-war school. It was from Hellingly that Mr Crook obtained much of the foundation stock for the Tiddicar kennels which flourished up to the outbreak of the second world war. His best known stud was Ch. Ajax of Hellingly.

Had the Olivers been able to sustain the high level of capital expenditure which they lavished on the kennels, I feel that even with the second world war, things would not have been as disastrous for the mastiff. With his wide circle of wealthy, and very influential friends, I am sure that Mr Oliver could have passed some mastiffs into safe keeping. Events proved otherwise and in January 1939 in the era of uneasy peace, E. G. Oliver died at his Yorkshire home of Bedale Hall under unusual circumstances, having apparently fallen downstairs and broken his neck. As the result of his sudden death, and subsequent evidence of the highly irregular procedures within his practice, of which his partner claimed to have been unaware, Hellingly was disbanded, and everything auctioned to repay creditors. Some of the mastiffs found their way to Canada and the very considerable collection of paintings, prints and books on the breed was dispersed.

Mrs Oliver left the dog scene and severed all connections with her wide circle of canine associates, and with the loss of its main force, and the outbreak of war, the death knell was sounded for the Mastiff Breeders Association. Many who had been members, or were closely associated with its running chose to dissociate themselves with the organisation after the daily press had given full coverage to the case. In 1969 I asked the late C. A. Binney, then Secretary of the Kennel Club, if there were records of the numerous trophies which the Association once owned. The Kennel Club had no such records, neither would they consider the reforming of the Association under its original constitution owing to the long lapse of time.

It would be uncharitable to dismiss E. G. Oliver because of the adverse publicity of 1939. The main interest of the case lay not so much in his deception, but rather in the high ranking positions of those deceived. He brought an enthusiasm and verve to mastiff affairs and was determined to give the breed publicity in what he considered to be the right sphere. In his after

A collection of mastiffs at the 'Tiddicar' kennels of Mr Crook. Photograph taken in the 1930s.

dinner speeches – and he was a first class speaker – he outlined the mastiff cause wherever possible, and insisted: 'We must be careful to look to our breeding and aim at type and soundness. It must be our object to eliminate such faults that there are. We must breed the best that it is possible to produce'.

Before Hitler managed to almost extinguish the mastiff flame, there were a few flickerings which were to burst into flame post-war. A Swiss restaurateur in Worcestershire, M. E. Perrenoud, purchased a mastiff in the mid thirties as guard for his premises. The dog was called Buller and died during the war, but left a deep impression on the owner.

Mr F. Bowles, sensing national disaster, sent a few of his Mansatta mastiffs for safe keeping in America. In 1938 Mrs P. Day was given a mastiff puppy as a Christmas present from her sister. He was bred by Mr L. Crook and mostly Hellingly in bloodline.

The long, hot summer of uneasy peace broke when Neville Chamberlain announced that Britain was at war with Germany. The pattern of life was suddenly disrupted. Owners fearing that they would be unable to feed such large dogs in wartime had them destroyed, and for the next five years, breeding operations in what was already a numerically weak breed ceased. Europe was at war.

The Post-War Crisis

When the war clouds finally cleared, victorious Britain found itself in economic difficulties and an unexpected social revolution. The unemployment of the 1920s and 1930s were still in the minds of many of those who returned. This, and the utter futility and waste of war swung the electorate towards socialism. It was an age when there was a new order for most things, but the older generation had doubts about the future. Those who had been able to support kennels of the giant breeds before the war were apprehensive, but despite all the changes there was a return to a more rational, if considerably altered way of life. The world of dogs began to rouse itself from war-imposed inactivity, and breeding got under way. A limited number of shows appeared in the calendar. As we saw in the previous section, the pre-war mastiff was not numerically strong, and the 1939 collapse of the Hellingly kennel had been a blow to its strength. When in 1945 an attempt was made to take stock of the mastiff in Britain, it became alarmingly clear that the war had decimated the breed far more seriously than was first supposed. Mrs Dicken remained as Secretary of the Old English Mastiff Club, which, although small at that time, still enjoyed the support of many pre-war specialists. Having become aware of the plight of the breed, Mrs Dicken made every effort to trace any known mastiff in Britain. She found that at the end of 1947 the total number of known mastiffs in Britain was seven. In the USA, which had been importing mastiffs since 1880, the position was little better than our own. Mr and Mrs Scheerboom's stock was old, and Miss Bell's had not survived the war. The Club, with commendable enterprise, called a public meeting at a London hotel with an invitation to anyone interested in the breed to attend and discuss measures of resuscitation.

From this meeting came the foundation of post-war mastiff breeding. Mrs P. Day brought her dog Hermit of Tiddicar who had been her inseparable companion in the war years. The late McDonald Daly, a journalist always on the look out for a good dog story, wrote an impassioned article in the *Sunday Express* giving the breed's plight full coverage. Miss Fawell brought a brindled dog to the meeting of unknown age or pedigree but presumed to be a mastiff. He had been rescued following an air raid at Eastbourne, and Miss Fawell had adopted the dog. Three championship show judges, one of them being Mr A. Croxton Smith, Chairman of the Kennel Club had certified him as being a mastiff and sanctioned his registration as Templecombe Taurus at the Kennel Club.

The name Taurus was engraved on the dog's collar when he was picked up in the street, but there were no other details. His registration was of 'pedigree, age and breeder unknown'.

There is considerable evidence that Templecombe Taurus was not a mastiff, but as the history of the mastiff so often records 'a mastiff with a dash of bull blood'. Whatever he was, the dog was of prime importance in the long and uphill struggle to prevent the extinction of the mastiff.

In 1959 I wrote an article in *Our Dogs* on colour inheritance in post war mastiffs mentioning Templecombe Taurus and querying his registration as a mastiff. An interesting reply came from Mr E. Christian, a resident of Eastbourne at that time, who wrote:

In October 1939 a two-year old black brindle bitch came into my care. There were two previous owners, and I could not obtain her pedigree until about nine months later. The second owner was under the impression that she was a bullmastiff. When her pedigree was to hand my suspicions were confirmed. The bitch was a pure mastiff. She was twenty-nine inches at the shoulder and weighed one hundred and seventy-five pounds; she was light in bone, very sound and active. Her sire was Bayard of Deleval (Ch. Cedric of Ashenhurst line) out of Gundreda of Deleval. In the meanwhile I had a litter from her by the bullmastiff Burngreave Baron, and she produced six puppies of which one was a dog. They were born in January 1940 and I retained the dog puppy, a brindle, and called him Taurus. I did not register him and he was my constant companion until October 1941 when I left home for military service. A friend gave him a home, and later he became attached to an A.A. unit which meant that I lost touch with him but the unit moved about the South East coastal area. After the war I learned that he was in good hands, and that the Kennel Club were interested in him. I took no action other than saying that his pedigree details were available to any interested party who chose to get in touch with me. I feel quite sure that this is the dog which you have in mind, and I can assure you of the correctness of its history. Taurus inherited his dam's mastiff characteristics but the heavier bone and masculine outlook of his bullmastiff sire.

The breeder's description certainly fits the dog, and the area in which he was found would tie up with that in which the unit was based. If, as I suspect, Taurus was this half-bred mastiff, he was probably invaluable at the time as he would have infused a little hybrid vigour.

A bitch was discovered in Essex bred in 1943 by Mrs E. Park, and carrying the pre-war Havengore line originating from Crescent Rowena. She was the product of a son to dam mating, the son being Robin of Brunwins, and the dam Hortia. The bitch was subsequently sold to Mrs L. J. Head and registered in 1944 as Sally of Coldblow. Mrs Head mated her to Templecombe Taurus in 1946 and from that mating came the keystone of Britain's post-war mastiffs, Nydia of Frithend, born 26 January 1947. Ocky White of Haverfordwest who had a pre-war interest in the mastiff bought Nydia's litter brother and sister which he registered as Ockite Wattaboy and Ockite Wattagirl, but both died of hardpad some months after their purchase.

In 1947 Mrs Dicken decided to go personally to the USA in the hope of locating, and purchasing stock, but her mission was fruitless. When one considers that club membership at that time was a mere twenty-nine, the efforts which this small organisation made were remarkable. In the meanwhile Major K. Hulbert of Fritham Grange, near Lyndhurst, Hants. had imported a brindled dog from the USA called Valiant Diadem. Major Hulbert was an authority on thoroughbred horses and had seen the dog when on a business trip to the States in connection with horses. Valiant Diadem went back to the Hellingly and Havengore bloodlines, and as Major Hulbert had by then purchased Nydia of Frithend, Diadem was imported as a suitable mate for her. To say that it was a fruitful union is an understatement, as the number of litters which these two produced was very large. Major Hulbert said that somehow

Diadem either managed to break down the door or squeeze through a partition whenever Nydia was on heat.

Mr F. Bowles imported some of his Mansatta line, which he had sent out to the USA at the beginning of hostilities. Realising the necessity of an outcross to get lines going, he mated one of his mastiff bitches to a large bullmastiff called Tawny Lion, owned by Mrs Shelley. According to his records he registered the stock as cross-breds and retained them, but if he bred from them at all, registrations are not recorded. Of the many good post-war dogs from Mansatta, his Ch. Vilna of Mansatta remains as the epitome of mastiff type in my mind. Vilna was squarely built with the strength of a warhorse; I wish that I owned a bitch like her today. Mr Bowles later became the custodian of the OEMC's Heatherbelle Sterling Silver, but we must try to retain chronological order.

1948 found Mrs Day crossing the Atlantic in search for a mate for her now aged Hermit of Tiddicar. She purchased the fawn bitch Honey of Parkhurst but by an ill stroke of Fate, Hermit died whilst his owner was abroad. The dog became distressed by his owner's absence, as they had never been previously separated, and this was probably a contributory cause of his demise. Mrs Duke of Brechin Angus imported Heatherbelle Bearehills Rajah in 1951. Mrs Duke was a pre-war owner, having owned a Goring dog who survived the war and lived to the age of fifteen. Mrs Duke's generosity in giving quarantine to the imported Club mastiffs should not pass without mention.

The solution to Britain's post-war mastiff crisis occurred in 1949, when, on reading of the breed's plight in Britain, Mr and Mrs Mellish of Canada presented the Old English Mastiff Club with a pair of mastiff puppies with the request that when things improved a pair should be returned. It was then that the Kennel Club took the unprecedented step of allowing the Old English Mastiff Club to become breeders and to use OEMC as a prefix. By 1950 not only were the club successful as breeders, but both Mrs Day and Mr Bowles had bred mastiff litters, plus of course the many progeny of Valiant Diadem and Nydia of Frithend. At the end of 1950 it was estimated that there were fifty mastiffs in Britain, twenty-two of which were of an age which should have made them capable of breeding.

Mr Greenwood of the pre-war Hillcrest mastiffs took on the responsibility of rearing the Canadian import bitch puppy after quarantine. She was successfully mated and at this stage Miss I. Bell became her custodian. In Miss Bell's care a litter of twelve puppies were whelped on 13 August 1950, sired by Valiant Diadem. 1950 also became a boom year for OEMC recruitment with twenty new recruits bringing the total membership to fifty-nine. It was a time when persons well-known in other breeds became interested in the mastiff revival. Mr and Mrs Aberdeen of Sparry Newfoundlands, Mesdames Dunkels and Gamble of Breakstones Boxers, Mrs Harrild of Moonsfield Danes and Mrs Gaines of Gaystock Bostons all became involved with the breed. A new recruit whose enthusiasm for the breed was immense but short lived was Peter Korda, son of the film magnate Sir Alexander Korda, then married to the famous filmstar Merle Oberon. The two champions owned by Mr and Mrs Peter Korda were the brindled brothers Ch. Vyking Aethelwulf of Salyng and Ch. Wotan Vyking.

By 1953 registrations were such that challenge certificates were on offer at shows, Crufts, Blackpool, Richmond and Birmingham being chosen as the events to receive the honours. At Crufts Mrs Scheerboom's brindled Rodney of Havengore bred by Major Hulbert by Valiant Diadem out of Nydia of Frithend, won the dog challenge certificate, and subsequently went on to become the first post-war mastiff champion. The bitch challenge certificate went to Miss Bell's OEMC Prudence. Practically every winner at these early shows was by Valiant Diadem out of Nydia of Frithend, which emphasises the importance of these two mastiffs. Mrs Mayne of Calstock in Cornwall had imported another bitch from Canada; this was Heatherbelle Priscillas Martha who won a great many variety classes in the West Country and added a useful publicity. Mrs Mayne now lives in Australia and has again taken up the mastiff in that country.

Rodney of Havengore won his qualifying CC at Crufts in 1954, and Mrs Harrild's OEMC Countess qualified at the same show. Rodney's brother Wotan Vyking qualified later in the same year.

Valiant Diadem had also been used on Mrs Day's imported Honey of Parkhurst, and three dogs and a bitch were born by caesarian section in 1950. Hippolyta of Hollesley, a brindle and Horatius of Hollesley, a fawn, were retained.

Mrs Day planned to mate Hippolyta, when old enough, to Mrs Duke's Heatherbelle Bearehills Rajah. Borrowing half the village's petrol ration books for the journey in a somewhat ancient tourer, and accompanied by Miss Kendal, the trio set off for the long journey to Angus. As is so often the case when one has made tremendous effort, the bitch totally rejected the advances of the stud dog so it was decided to try the animals again the next day hoping that a night's rest would prove beneficial. The ladies stayed in an historic guest house, owned by an old Scottish family. An ancient claymore was lodged in an equally ancient tree near the house, and legend had it that when the claymore fell to the ground the family would die out. Perhaps Hippolyta sensed the aura of doom, as she returned from Scotland unmated, and by a twist of fate her line died out, although she later produced a litter to Heatherbelle Sterling Silver.

Mr M. E. Perrenoud re-entered the mastiff world in 1951 and purchased Withybush Beatrix from Miss Bell. Beatrix was by Rodney of Havengore out of OEMC Heatherbelle Portia of Goring. Mr Perrenoud then registered his Meps prefix taking his young son and daughter as partners in the prefix. I well remember Beatrix and her youthful handler. Beatrix was very sound, typey, free moving and almost a fox red in colour. She won her first CC at Richmond in 1955 under Mr Greenwood, her second at Blackpool under Mr F. J. Hawkings in 1957 and would have become a champion had she been further campaigned, but Mr Perrenoud withdrew her from shows after her second CC and concentrated on mastiff breeding.

Miss I. Bell imported a dog whose name still regularly crops up in pedigrees from Mrs H. Weyenburgh in the USA. This import was Weyacres Lincoln, a silver fawn son of Withybush Magnus (which Miss Bell had bred here and exported to the USA) out of Peachfarm Priscilla; it is through his son Jason of Copenore that his name still appears. Miss Bell pinned great faith in this dog who certainly had size, a very typical head and an impressive front with ample bone. One of his early and important sons was the brindle Ch. Withybush Aethelred, whose head was one of the best in the ring at that time. Aethelred inherited his sire's reliable temperament, but both dogs in my opinion (and I watched them from the ringside on many occasions) lacked a decisive hind action. Miss Bell was a very clever handler, although not young to be showing such heavy dogs; but neither of the dogs ever seemed to get into their stride behind. The same applied to Withybush Crispin, a fine head, and true mastiff outlook, but lacking in drive of the hindquarters. It is probable that Miss Bell had long term plans for improving the hindquarters and was at that time consolidating the many qualities which her line possessed. A breeder of her experience would certainly have been aware of points which needed strengthening on a long term basis, but one must remember that at this stage the mastiff was only just emerging from its near extinction and the fact that one had any breeding material with which to work was rather miraculous.

The first litter bred by the Perrenouds was in 1953 when Withybush Beatrix produced a litter of twelve to her grandfather Valiant Diadem, and seven and a half months later another twelve puppies by Ch. Vyking Aethelwulf of Salyng. In this litter were two brindles, Meps Basil and Meps Berenice, the latter

Withybush Beatrix (2 CCs, 2 reserve CCs). Owners: M. E., M. E. Jnr and Miss M. E. Perrenoud. Born 1951.

USA. Ch. Meps Berenice, born May 1954. Breeders: Meps Kennels, Worcester. Owner: Mrs Marie A. Moore, USA. Handler: Mr P. Gordon Banton. The first post-war bitch champion in USA. The first mastiff to obtain champion title in 15 years (1956).

exported to Mrs Marie Moore to become America's first post-war mastiff champion bitch. Meps Basil was to be exported to the same owner at a later date, but due to a breakdown in the arrangements, Mrs Moore who had purchased him presented him to Mrs Dickin. This was at a time when Mrs Dickin had a few Border Terriers and did not feel disposed to taking the dog herself but arranged with Mrs Scheerboom to give Basil a home for life, although he remained the property of Mrs Dickin. Meps Basil repaid his

Ch. Hotspot of Havengore.

caretaker handsomely by siring in 1958 what was undoubtedly the greatest post-war mastiff, Ch. Hotpot of Havengore.

Another fortunate purchase for the Meps Kennels was the bitch Cora of Wormhill, who was by Valiant Diadem out of Nydia of Frithend. Cora had been sold to the well-known bullmastiff fancier Vic Smith by Jack Barnard, whose early bullmastiff breeding, although of importance, was eclipsed by his pioneering work for the Staffordshire Bull Terrier under the Chestonian prefix. Vic Smith offered Cora to me prior to advertising her but at the time I was fully committed with bullmastiffs, and having no spare kennel to house her, turned the offer down. It was later discovered that Cora appeared to be a non-breeder as both previous owners had failed to get a litter from her. When Mr Perrenoud purchased her he mated her to Meps Jumbo of Mansatta, a stud dog then in the kennels which he had purchased from Mr F. Bowles. A litter of nine resulted.

By the late 1950s the two most numerous kennels were those of Mrs Scheerboom and Miss Bell. It must have been gratifying to Mrs Scheerboom to know that the post-war revival was based on her pre-war Havengore stock. Mrs Scheerboom's long experience in the breed had given her decided ideas on type and the aim had always been on soundness and a broad, stocky mastiff with square skull and strong muzzle. The latter point was as much a feature in Ch. Hotspot as it had been in the pre-war Ch. Bill of Havengore. In my opinion one of the best pairs of mastiffs doing the show rounds in the latter part of the 1950 decade were Mrs Scheerboom's Ch. Diann of Havengore and Mr W. Hanson's Ch. Drake of Havengore. Diann was the epitome of

Havengore type, broad, sound, wide and deep chested. Some considered that Drake could have been larger all over, which is fair criticism but this solid soundly moving brindle was to my mind little short of the ideal. These two animals took top honours at Birmingham City in 1958, repeated the perform-ance at Richmond under Mrs France (nee Greenwood) and at LKA under Mrs Day all in the same year. Ch. Drake was the spark that kindled Mr Hanson's interest in the breed and later blossomed into the Blackroc prefix which (to Britain's disadvantage) ended up in America.

The breed suffered two sad occurences in 1959 and 1960. M. E. Perrenoud died suddenly in 1959 and the kennels disbanded. At the time of his death there were fifty-five mastiffs (including puppies) and in the two years preceed-ing his death there were never less than fourteen mastiffs in the kennels.

Miss Bell died on 30 November 1960, leaving her mastiffs to Miss P. M. Blackstone on the understanding that any over the age of eighteen months would be destroyed. This very difficult decision had been taken some years previously and both her solicitor and the veterinary surgeon were well aware of these wishes. At the time of her death there were twenty-two dogs and bitches in the kennels, fourteen of which were over the age of eighteen months together with some puppies. Miss P. M. and her sister Miss B. Blackstone decided to keep the dog Withybush Superbus, a brindle, and two young bitches, Mrs Hector joining them in the venture. Mrs Hector had owned a pair

Mrs E. Harrild, Judge at Birmingham City championship show, 1958.
Left: Mr F. Scheerboom with Ch. Diann of Havengore. Right: Mr W. Hanson
with Ch. Drake of Havengore. Both exhibits bred by Mrs L. Scheerboom.

The OEMC first post-war championship show at Pangbourne Nautical college.
Fifty-seven mastiffs were entered for Mrs N. Dicken to judge.
Left to right: Miss Willis with Cherry of Havengore; Mrs Lewis with Bardayle
Stroma of Stoam; Mrs P. Day with Ch. Dawn of Havengore; Mr W. Hanson with
Gipsy of Havengore; Mrs L. Scheerboom with Louise of Havengore (winner of
2 CCs).

of Deleval mastiffs before the war, and post-war had made up Ch. Olwen of
Parcwood a daughter of Weyacres Lincoln. The litter of puppies was already
booked, and she was therefore spared, and Mr and Mrs Munn, who had
helped Miss Bell in the kennels and garden, asked if they could have the dam
of the litter as she was their favourite mastiff. This was agreed by the solicitors
and executors.

The Misses Blackstone attempted to continue Miss Bell's lines and Withybush
Superbus was used at stud; in fact I own a brindle today who goes back to him
and probably inherits his colour from him.

There were comments after Miss Bell's death that her action in having the
dogs destroyed was somewhat irresponsible when one considers the still
precarious numerical strength of the breed. It is a point of view to which I do
not subscribe. Some older dogs settle in homes if they have been previously
housed in kennels, but I should be very reluctant to part with any dog of mine
over the age of two, except to persons intimately known to me. When one
considers Miss Bell's long mastiff association it must have been a very difficult
decision for her to reach, and one admires her courage in implementing it.

Miss Bell's family were military, and although during the war agricultural
participation was forced on Great Withybush, Miss Bell was not an agriculturist

as such, though she owned, and bred, Shetland ponies. The Withybush prefix was a post-war innovation; her pre-war dogs were not registered under a prefix. In 1958 a young mastiff dog was presented by the OEMC to the forty-seventh Guided Weapons Regiment as their mascot. He became Gunner Thor and was paraded on important occasions.

In 1958 the OEMC held its first post-war mastiff show. It was at Pangbourne, and Mrs Dickin judged. The tide was definitely turning for the breed and there was a steady influx of new breeders. The late 1950s saw Mr S. R. Anderson developing a mastiff strain under his Lexander prefix. Having made up Ch. Drake of Havengore Mr Hanson took on the brindled bitch Gipsey of Havengore. Mrs A. Anderson of the Bardayle prefix was active, and had considerable pre-war experience, as she used then to take charge of a mastiff in the absence of his owners. Mr and Mrs Lindley were expanding the Copenore kennels to the considerable importance which they became in later years. Copenore must hold the breed record for having bred more champions for their clients than for themselves. Mrs Lindley had to wait for more than ten years before making up her first Copenore champion. This was Ch. Copenore Mary Ellen, yet puppies and stock sold from Copenore had made deep inroads into the showing.

Mrs Scheerboom's Ch. Hotspot of Havengore was the invincible show dog of the era. Before he was three years old he had won ten CCs, two reserve CCs and ten best of breed awards. Hotspot was a typical mastiff, broad, long backed, heavily boned and strongly muscled. He had the strength and square-ness of skull and muzzle which had always been Mrs Scheerboom's aim. His critics said that he showed enough haw and that his colour was too inclined towards red to be correctly described as apricot, but these were trifling criticisms when one compares them with the superb quality of this dog.

The 1960s brought more new recruits to the breed such as Mrs I. Creigh whose Kisumu prefix was well known and often successful in the show ring. Mr Hanson's Ch. Falcon of Blackroc qualified in the USA for his new owner Mrs Marie Moore, thus becoming an international champion. His fawn brother Rhinehart of Blackroc was also purchased by Mrs Moore, who in a letter to me some years ago said that, although Falcon may have been the better specimen, Rhinehart sired the better stock. Had these dogs stayed here and been used at stud I think that the breed in this country would have benefitted.

A dog whose influence has been left in the breed is Ch. Balint of Havengore owned by Mr and Mrs I. Monostori and bred by Mr A. Anderson. He was by Ch. Hotspot of Havengore out of Cindy Lou of Bardayle. If for no other reason Balint will be remembered as the sire of Ch. Meps Portia and her brother Ch. Gelert of Pynes Farm. Ch. Meps Portia, who marked the return to the mastiff ring of Miss Perrenoud, had a remarkable show career, and was retired from the show ring unbeaten by any other bitch. In her only litter she produced Ch. Meps Nydia who was somewhat short lived, and the American Champion Meps Tristan, a prolific sire in the USA.

A very strong kennels of the era, and fortunately still very much in action was Nantymynydd of Mrs A. Davies, near Tregaron Dyfed. Returning to her native Wales from the Far East, Mrs Davies decided not only to return to her

*International champion Falcon of Blackroc. Owner: Mrs Marie Moore, USA.
Breeder W. Hanson.*

Ch. Balint of Havengore at 20 months of age. Owner: Mrs S. Monostori.

much-loved country, but to an equally loved breed. Many years previously she had owned a mastiff which she had saved from ill-treatment on a farm, but her childhood days had been spent with the mother's bullmastiffs which were of the old mastiffy type.

The cornerstone of her breeding was the brindled bitch Catherine of Copenore, purchased from Mrs Creigh. Catherine mated to Ch. Balint of Havengore produced the fawn Emrys O Nantymynydd, one of the soundest mastiffs which I have ever seen, and one who transmitted that soundness. My introduction to this dog was a bounding leap over the settee and back again with the effortless manner of a steeplechaser. He was as sound in temperament as he was in limb, and it was probably the subsequent inbreeding to this dog that gave Nantymynydd dogs better movement than most. The prefix is well known in the USA and some of the continental mastiffs were founded on Nantymynydd stock. Mrs Davies is virtually a non-exhibitor and after a period of inactivity I am pleased to say that at the time of writing the kennels have been rebuilt with stock from her old Emrys line. A pleasant day was recently

Ch. Meps Portia. Breeder: T. H. Bradley. Born 1968. Owner: Miss M. E. Perrenoud. Winner of eight CCs including 'best of breed' Crufts. Retired unbeaten. The first mastiff to win the K.C. Junior Warrant.

Mrs A. Davies's Mab Myfanwy o Nantymynydd. Note the square head, widely spaced eyes and strong muzzle.

spent at Tregaron watching these dogs moving up and down the slopes in great style. There was a particularly interesting collection of young brindles, as this is the colour long associated with the establishment.

Another Welsh fancier is Mr R. Cogan who used to work part time as a kennel boy for Ocky White in pre-war days. Mr Cogan has made up a champion but the one I most admired was his Taddington Emma, a stocky short-loined mastiff who won her second CC at the age of eight, and although she did not get her qualifying certificate, remained active and healthy until over eleven years of age.

Having lost her Parkhurst line, Mrs Day's sister again presented her with a mastiff puppy, this time from Havengore. She was Dawn of Havengore who was by Turk of Havengore out of Sally Anne of Havengore. Dawn was the perfect guard, but sworn enemy of her litter sister, Hanson's Gipsy of Havengore. Perhaps this was colour prejudice as Dawn was fawn and Gipsy brindle, but whenever these two met in the show ring they showed their dislike for one another. Dawn, when mated to Jason of Copenore, produced Ch. Macushla of Hollesley, the winner of sixteen CCs, and a bitch record holder by Crufts on three occasions, 1966, 1969, 1970, the last two also being best of breed wins. Macushla's son Ch. Hollesley Macushla Dagda, owned by Mrs E. Degerdon, helped to keep the line alive, chiefly through his son Ch. Copenore Rab. Mrs Degerdon's mastiff ownership dates back to the 1950s and the present kennel was built up using the Ch. Copenore Rab line and the American

73

imported Ch. Devil from Wayside line. The latter dog was particularly sound in hindquarters and did much to rectify a long standing mastiff weakness. The fact that he carried Dogue de Bordeaux far back in his pedigree seemed to alarm some, but I think that anyone who has reached this stage of the book will realise that such crossings are not exactly unknown in the breed and in many cases have proved to be beneficial.

Under the Jilgrajon prefix Mrs W. and Mr J. Hicks have shown a dedication to all things mastiff. Mr J. Hicks was the first director of the rescue scheme and worked endlessly in that capacity. Their winning dogs have included Ch. Jilgrajon Lady Victoria, Ch. Jilgrajon Sir Gladstone who was top mastiff for 1981, Ch. Caemes King Edward of Jilgrajon and the brindle Ch. Jilgrajon Rebecca West.

Mrs Norfolk's Celerity Kennels has also been a useful foundation for many, as the Celerity dogs are invariably sound. Mesdames Lloyd Jones and Greenwell

Gwyliwr-O-Nantymynydd (born 1971), bred by Mrs A. Davies, owner Mrs S. Monostori. Study the standard, and apply it to this dog. There is nothing of the bullmastiff, Great Dane or Newfoundland here. This is the correct length of back and the overall type for which we should aim. Photograph taken at 9 months.

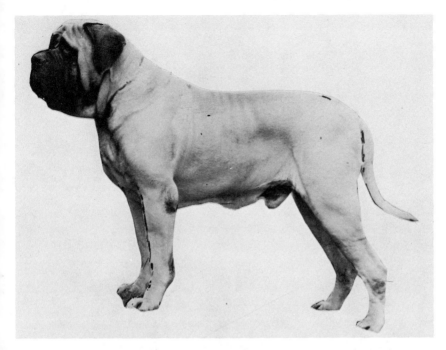

Ch. Hollesley Medicine Man, owned by Mesdames Lloyd-Jones and Greenwell. Medicine Man holds the record for the number of CCs won by a dog and was the sire of champions.

have had a long association with the breed, and their Ch. Hollesley Medicine Man has had an exceptional show career winning the Crufts CC on three consecutive occasions and now holds the record for the highest number of CCs won by any mastiff. One of his early progeny, Miss Atkinson's Ch. Honeycroft Danny Boy, had the distinction of gaining his title whilst still a junior.

Mrs E. J. Baxter's Farnaby prefix is of long standing and is strongly associated with brindles; in fact, her first mastiff was the brindle Ch. Taddington Diamond Lil of Farnaby, and many of the brindled Farnaby dogs go back to her. The litter sisters Ch. Yarme Jane of Farnaby and Ch. Yarme Susan of Farnaby were of first class type, as was Ch. Farnaby Arabella. Mr Baxter's Farnaby Alice of Shute, a fawn who epitomised mastiff type, was very unlucky not to have gained her title as she was of such quality. Alice produced only one litter but in that litter was Lesdon The Lord Alexander, my old brindle who lies beside me as I type this manuscript. The latest Farnaby champion is Ch. Parcwood Sir W. Bear of Lesdon, bred by Mrs Hector, by Ch. Overnoons Mr Micawber of Buckhall out of Ch. Farnaby Rainy Patch. Perhaps one should add that Mr D. Baxter owns the Lesdon prefix but dogs of both prefixes are housed in the same kennels.

Mr and Mrs C. Say, who came into the breed after some years of bullmastiff ownership, have succeeded in producing mastiffs of a recognisable type,

The author's Jilgrajon Tom Bawling head-study, taken at 20 months, shows the correct stop and skull/muzzle proportions.

Ch. Parcwood, W. Bear, Esq. of Lesdon. Owner: Mr D. Baxter. This dog features in many of today's pedigrees.

Ch. Bulliff Warrior. Born 1983. Breeders and owners: Mr and Mrs C. Say. Warrior has twice been 'best of breed' at Crufts, including 1987.

Mr R. Boatwright with his Ch. Glynpedr Taittinger. An informal shot taken at a summer show.

including champions. Their original President of Shute was litter brother to Alice of Shute, mentioned previously. President is the keystone of the Bulliff dogs and whilst I have not checked the records with the owners, feel that there are few, if any, in their kennel that do not stem from him.

To bring mastiff developments up to date, we have had an influx of new breeders such as Messers Tugwell and Thomas, and Mr R. Boatwright who are keen exhibitors, and have had a run of success in this sphere. We also have as new exhibitors Mr and Mrs McDonald who to date have made up two champions and are loyal supporters of mastiff classes throughout Britain. Mrs M. Joynes of Newport made up the first mastiff which she bought as a puppy, Ch. Celerity Powerful Sort, and then repeated this with his daughter Ch. Zanfi Princess Tanya of Damaria.

The Old English Mastiff Club is numerically stronger than at any time in its long history, and in 1983 held its centenary show at Pyleigh Court Farm, Taunton. The one fact about which we can all be assured is that due to its present strength both in Britain and abroad, the breed will never again find itself in the state of near extinction into which it had fallen in 1947.

Mr R. Boatwright's Ch. Zanfi Imperial Eagle of Glynpeda. Breeder: Mr N. Waters.

Messrs Thomas and Tugwell's Ch. Forefoot King Kong. Note the excellent head type and overall balance of this quality dog.

Messrs Thomas and Tugwell's Ch. Bredwardine Beau Ideal. Bred by owners, this bitch holds the all-time record for number of cc's won.

Mr and Mrs E. Jones's, champion Faerdorn Big Daddy, winner of six CC's, five times 'best of breed'. Reserve in working group, Birmingham Dog Show Society, championship show, May 1984.

Mrs E. Hudson with 'Golden Madonna of Tmaramara' at Clearwell Castle show,
1980. Note the wonderful conformation of this young exhibit, especially the excellent
shoulder placement.
Photo: R. C. Beddis.

Mrs M. Joynes's Damaria the Chieftain (photograph taken at 10 months old).

Mrs M. Joyne's Ch. Zanfi Princess Tanya of Damaria (born 1981). Breeder: Mr N. Waters. Sire: Celerity Powerfull Sort. Dam: Grangemoor Gilda.

USA. Mr and Mrs Korn's Ch. Autumn River Big Ben Breeder, V. G. Bregman (1982). Sire: Lazy Hill Luath. Dam: Ch: Lazy Hill Athena. The author made this dog 'best of breed' when judging Bucks. County Kennel Club, 1986. This dog has the correct head-type and true mastiff substance and bone. His height comes not from length of leg, but his tremendous depth of body, which is what one should aim at in the breed. Note the front and depth of brisket in this fine specimen.
Photo: Tatham.

7

The Mastiff Breed Standard and its appraisal

The Mastiff Breed Standard

General Appearance

Large, powerful, symmetrical and well knit frame. A combination of grandeur and good nature, courage and docility. The head is general outline giving square appearance when viewed from any point. Breadth greatly to be desired, and should be in ratio to length of the whole head and face as 2 to 3. Body massive, broad, deep, long, powerfully built on legs wide apart and squarely set. Muscles sharply defined. Size a great desideratum if combined with quality. Height and substance important if both points are proportionately combined.

Head and Skull

Skull broad between the ears, forehead flat, but wrinkled when attention is excited. Brows (superciliary ridges) slightly raised. Muscles of the temples and cheeks (temperal and masseter), well developed. Arch across the skull of a rounded, flattened curve, with a depression up the centre of the forehead from the median line between the eyes, to halfway up the sagittal suture. Face or muzzle short, broad under the eyes, and keeping nearly parallel in width to the end of the nose; truncated, i.e. blunt and cut off squarely, thus forming a right angle with the upper line of the face, of great depth from the point of the nose to the underjaw. Under jaw broad to the end. Nose broad, with widely spreading nostrils when viewed from the front, flat (not pointed or turned up) in profile. Lips diverging at obtuse angles with the septum, and slightly pendulous so as to show a square profile. Length of muzzle to whole head and face as 1 to 3. Circumference of muzzle (measured midway between the eyes and nose) to that of the head (measured before the ears) as 3 to 5.

Eyes

Small, wide apart, divided by the space of at least two eyes. The stop between the eyes well marked, but not too abrupt. Colour hazel brown, the darker the better, showing no haw.

Ears

Small, thin to the touch, wide apart, set on at the highest points of the sides of the skull, so as to continue the outline across the summit, and lying flat and close to the cheeks when in repose.

Mouth
Canine teeth healthy, powerful and wide apart; incisors level, or the lower projecting beyond the upper but never so much as to become visible when the mouth is closed.

Neck
Slightly arched, moderately long, very muscular and measuring in circumference about one or two inches less than the skull before the ears.

Forequarters
Shoulder and arm slightly sloping, heavy and muscular. Legs straight, strong and set wide apart, bones being large. Elbows square. Pasterns upright.

Body
Chest wide, deep and well let down between forelegs. Ribs arched and well rounded. False ribs deep, and well set back to the hips. Girth should be one third more than the height at the shoulder. Back and loins wide and muscular; flat and very wide in a bitch, slightly arched in a dog. Great depth of flanks.

Hindquarters
Broad, wide and muscular, with well developed second thighs, hocks bent, wide apart and quite squarely set when standing, or walking.

Feet
Large and round. Toes well arched up. Nails black.

Tail
Put on high up, and reaching to the hocks or a little below them. Wide at its root and tapering to the end, hanging straight in repose, but forming a curve with the end pointing upwards but not over the back, when the dog is excited.

Coat
Short and close lying, but not too fine over the shoulders, neck and back.

Colour
Apricot, silver fawn, or dark fawn brindle. In any case, muzzle, ears and nose should be black with black round the orbits, and extending upwards between them.

An Appraisal of the Mastiff Breed Standard

There are few breed standards as specific in detail as that of the mastiff, yet its translation and application is the subject of much contention and variation. The general description is for a dog which is 'large, massive, powerful, with well knit frame'. It will be noted that in the British standard heights either minimum or maximum are not mentioned as such; therefore anything approaching the narrow Dane type cannot be typical. In America a minimum height is quoted, which to me is something of a retrograde step, as it has probably led to the misconception that a tall dog is a large dog. It may not be. Size has a dimension other than height, yet too often a mastiff lacking breadth but possessing height is considered typical when in fact it is not. No narrow chested animal could be accurately described as 'massive'; it therefore lacks a fundamental requirement.

The body girth should be one third greater than the height at the shoulder. If this is considered in conjunction with the requirement that the body shall be broad, deep, long, powerfully built on legs wide apart and squarely set, it is obvious that height is relatively unimportant. When the standard was originally drawn up in 1883, the committee wanted a long-bodied, heavy, broad dog probably as a reaction against the boarhound types which were found in the early mastiffs.

Let us now consider the implications of the requirement that 'size is a great desideratum if combined with quality'. No one wishes to see miniature mastiffs, but what were the pioneers saying, and as we are supposed to be breeding and judging to the standard, how do we translate it?

Does the standard say in effect 'Make quality, not immense size your aim'? We all know that the bigger the dog the greater the chances are of unsoundness. Nature appears to have well defined limits, and when those limits are exceeded things start to go wrong. If one looks again at the wording of the standard, a judge could, or even should, place a smaller animal which combines this quality with the specified proportions, over one which is much larger, but is lacking in quality. However one views the standard, what is undeniable is that the dog shall be massive, broad-chested, the body to be long and deep, and this heavy body to be carried on four strong legs. It is obvious that the narrow, poorly boned, or weedy, fail in the main essentials.

Head and skull
As this is the most detailed part of the standard, one presumes that it is the most important. The requirements are spelt out in detail, but can be summarised as broad between the ears, muzzle short and broad beneath the eyes, and cut off squarely. The lips are to be slightly pendulous to give the necessary overall squareness, the nose broad, with well spread nostrils. To summarise, the head should be square when viewed from all angles. The ears are required to be set on the highest points of the sides of the skull so as to continue the outline of the summit.

This is a précis of the requirements, but from it we can identify several prevalent faults. The bloodhoundy head with domed skull and low set ears is quite obviously wrong, as is the weak muzzled. So is the skull which has a tendency to roundness, which is getting quite common in the breed. It may be of interest to note that the standard does not mention 'wrinkle', except for asking that the flat forehead should be wrinkled when the attention is excited. Is this not saying that there should be little or no wrinkle on the forehead (or anywhere else) when the dog is in repose? Excessive wrinkle is therefore a fault if present when the dog is in repose, yet I have seen winners with skin hanging in folds over the major part of the head described as having a 'typical and expressive head'.

We have a multiplicity of head types in the breed today, some verging on the Bullmastiff, and on the other extreme some heads far too similar to that of a Great Dane. There are some with a great deal of ropey wrinkle, which would be an asset on a Mastino Napoletano, but is quite out of place on a mastiff.

The set of the ear can make a great deal of difference to a dog's expression. The low-set, houndy ear is often accompanied by a domed skull and the doleful expression of a bloodhound. Many ears are too large, and too thick as well as being the wrong colour. The small, thin, black ear is becoming something of a rarity yet is distinctly asked for in the standard.

Body
Ribs arched and well rounded false ribs well set back to the hips. A prevalent fault in mastiffs of the last century, and the early twentieth century was the

Mastiff Head faults. 1. The correct type and expression. 2. Long houndy ears, eyes too closely set. 3. Domed skull and low-set ears. 4. Overwrinkled skull and excessive loose skin about the throat. 5. Lacking in stop long, and weak in muzzle. Whilst one does not want excessive wrinkle, this head is far too plain and Dane like.

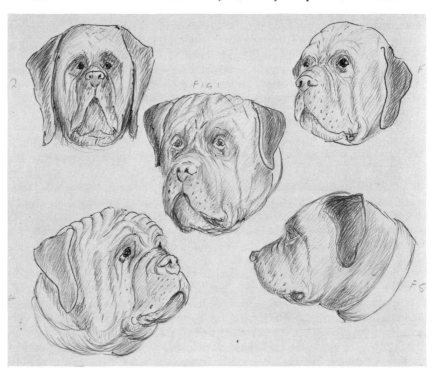

weak dipping back caused by a long slack loin. The standard's requirement has been carefully thought out and is sound canine anatomy but seems to be misunderstood. I have often heard experienced breeders, and some judges say 'I don't like long backs in any breed, they are always weak', so let us look briefly at the requirement.

The ribs are connected to the twelve dorsal vertebrae, the thirteen lumbar vertebrae are not supported by the ribs. The ideal arrangement for a mastiff is for the dorsal vertebrae to be long, and the lumbar vertebrae to be short. In such an arrangement not only is the spine well supported, but the longer rib cage gives greater lung space. It is comparatively easy to check the length of the lumbar vertebrae as it is roughly the distance between the last rib and the prominences at the upper end of the pelvis. I always check this distance when judging as if the lumbar vertebrae are long not only is the rib cage likely to be inadequate, but the long loin can lead to weakness.

Forequarters and Hindquarters
Good muscular development is required by the standard. Muscle building and exercise are dealt with elsewhere in the book, but far too many mastiffs are shown with poor musculature chiefly due to lack of the correct exercise, and too close confinement. One should be able to see the muscular development of the second thigh, but this is not always the case. A proportion of otherwise satisfactory exhibits lack the width and depth of flank which is called for by the standard. A note on the second thigh and its function in movement is given in the appropriate section.

Coat
We have variations ranging from the too fine to the shaggy St Bernard type of coat. This long coat crops up in litters, but such dogs are not normally exhibited. The long coat factor is probably a recessive. A coat with the same density all over the body is incorrect. When one considers that the mastiff was for years a chained watchdog it would have been necessary to have a degree of weatherproofing over those parts of the body normally exposed to the elements. The shoulders, back and neck are obvious points requiring protection, hence the standard's requirement of the coat not being too fine over these parts.

Colour
The need for the black ear has already been mentioned, but the body colour gives choice. 'Apricot' is something of a misnomer as apricots are basically yellow, whereas many so-called 'apricot' mastiffs are in fact red fawns. Silver fawn is self explanatory but 'dark fawn brindle' is not so easily explained. Does the standard require dark fawn stripes on a blackish background, or black stripes on a dark fawn background? It is a question of interpetation, and either could be considered correct. Many feel that where a dog has large fawn areas which are devoid of brindle striping, such a colour is incorrect. The standard does not say so, and even this is a debatable point especially as there are those who say that, as with horses, 'a good dog cannot be a bad colour'. White

markings are sometimes seen on the feet and chest of brindles, and as long as these are small should not be excessively penalised.

Mouth
Canine teeth healthy, powerful, and wide apart, incisors level or the lower projecting beyond the upper but never so much as to be visible when the mouth is closed.

For the canine teeth to be set widely apart the jaw must be broad to the end, which is an obvious piece of geometry, but it is the second part of the requirement which is puzzling.

An undershot mouth is not a fault unless so badly undershot that, as in the bulldog, the lower incisors are visible when the mouth is closed. This certainly gives great latitude, and as the standard is worded, it is the literal translation, but is it the correct one? Any experienced judge does not need to pull back the lips to see whether or not the mouth is undershot, or the reverse. In some cases where the degree of undershot is greater than that called for in the standard, the front of the lower lip may protrude over the upper lip when the mouth is closed, but the teeth will still not be visible even though the jaw is undershot. I have often wondered whether what the pioneers had in mind was that the jutting lower jaw should not be visible when the mouth is closed, and to me this would make sense.

In my opinion a slightly undershot lower jaw enhances the determined expression which typifies the mastiff. On the other hand if the lower jaw is too undershot its jutting forward will deter from the standard's requirement of overall squareness of muzzle.

Eyes
Hazel brown in colour, the darker the better, small, set widely apart, showing no haw. Eye colour is hereditary, but in assessing eye colour some consideration should be given to the coat colour. Hazel eyes in a silver fawn would be acceptable but the same coloured eyes in a really dark brindle will look several degrees lighter. This is yet another reason why the true assessment of a brindle is more difficult than a fawn. The narrowly set eye gives a mean expression, and one needs a widely spaced almond-shaped eye to give the necessary intensity which epitomises the mastiff. One should never forget that the dogs were at one time fighting animals, so a deeper set small eye would not be as vulnerable to damage as a round eye, especially if it has the tendency to protrude.

Excessive haw spoils the expression and gives the mastiff a doleful, blood-hound look. It is not only aesthetically wrong, but physiologically wrong as the hanging and exposed mucous membranes become susceptible to infections. Pre-war mastiffs suffered with the reverse condition of entropion, when the eyelid and eyelashes turned in. This again is a hereditary condition but it can be alleviated by surgery. One should not consider surgery to be the answer to such problems, far better to try to breed away from the condition.

In conclusion, the interpetation of a breed standard is often a personal one. It is always possible for different individuals to read different meanings or emphasis into the same words. All that one hopes for is that everyone studies the standard and formulates an opinion on what it is attempting to say. A far greater appreciation will be achieved if one knows why the requirements were made in the first instance.

Holland. Lazybones Load Rab. A well-known winner on the Continent, owned by Miss Bine Blaauw.

Forefoot Theseus, owned by Hartwig Lohmann, Stonehage Kennels, Steinhagen, W. Germany.

Mr C. Eraclides's CC winner Alcama Zorba of La-Susa, born 1981. A combination of American and English bloodlines.

J. and D. Bahlman's Ch. Old Schools Panama Red. Winning 'best of winners award' in USA at 20 months.

USA. Ch. Deer Run Wycliff, owned by Messrs Jackson and Gibbs of Frenchtown, New Jersey, USA. Wycliff sired more champions than any mastiff stud dog in the world.

USA. Jackson & Gibbs of Deer Run Kennels. Successfully campaign Ch. Deer Run Ivan, son of the famous Ch. Deer Run Wycliff.

The author's homebred Wyaston Henry Tudor.
Photo: E. Alexander.

An interesting photograph from 1912. The child was a gamekeeper's daughter and the two dogs supposed to have been bullmastiffs of the pre-recognition era.

8

The Bullmastiff

History

A major part of bullmastiff history has already been covered in the mastiff section, but as the bullmastiff is so often considered to be a British breed of comparatively modern production, facts must be produced to refute the argument.

The Bull-Mastiff (as it was then written) was accepted by the Kennel Club as a pure breed in 1924, but it obviously occurred long before that date. It may have been called 'The Keeper's Night Dog', 'A Mastiff with a dash of Bull', 'a large Bulldog' or 'a smaller and mongrel mastiff' but an animal with bulldog and mastiff characteristics existed.

Craven in his *The Bull Mastiff as I know it* quotes an advertisement from the *Manchester Mercury* of 27 November 1785 which reads: 'Taken up on the road between Huddersfield and Marsden on Sunday 15 Nov. 1795 a large light coloured dog between the bull and mastiff kind'. In the first edition of *The Dogs of the British Islands* by Stonehenge there is a chapter devoted to 'The Keeper's Night Dog' and whilst it does not quote the bullmastiff as such, in later editions of the book, reference is made to bull crosses as 'chiefly with the mastiff as in the keeper's night dog'.

Rev. Wynn in his *History of the Mastiff* to which I have made frequent references earlier in the book makes significant references to the bullmastiff. The first is a quotation from a letter of Mr Thompson in 1873: 'I also called upon John Turner who informed me that there was a fine dog at Keighley which he proposed breeding from. He is by Bradford Quaker out of a large bull mastiff bitch. . . .'

An interesting reference to the bullmastiff which appears to have been overlooked by the breed historians may be found in Edward Jesse's *Anecdotes of dogs* (1846). In the introduction Jesse wrote: 'I had forgotten to mention a bull and mastiff dog that I once owned, called Grumbo . . .' The author then describes his youthful experiences with the dog whose willingness to take on combat seems somewhat typical.

The fact that the artist George Morland (1763–1801) painted a dog of the bullmastiff type on more than one occasion would suggest that such a type existed. There is always the possibility that this type of dog was the progenitor of both bulldog and mastiff. We have seen that the mid nineteenth century dogs were founded on foreign animals. Was Morland's dog a mastiff, or a bulldog? If one mistakenly believes that there was no such breed as a bullmastiff at that time what was the animal which Morland portrayed and on more than one occasion?

We could speculate for chapters and prove very little, but suffice it to say that before the Kennel Club's acceptance of the Bull Mastiff as a pure breed, dogs of bull and mastiff parentage existed. Such dogs were essentially working dogs and those who felt that a dash of Dane or St Bernard would enhance the abilities of their bull mastiff did the necessary crosses. The whole reason for the development of the bullmastiff was to evolve an animal with the guarding abilities of the mastiff, and the courage of the bulldog, but an animal with greater speed and agility than the mastiff proper.

Count V. Hollander writing in *The Kennel* March 1911 makes a plea for what he describes as 'An unrecognised breed of British dogs'. He writes: 'The public know very little of the qualities of the Bull-Mastiff and, what is more, that it has been in existence for some considerable time. It is useless to make an appeal for this dog from a sentimental point of view, I do so quite conscientiously knowing that this dog is the bravest, the most perfect guard and protector in the world'. Later in the article he writes: 'Mr Biggs of Osmaston Hall Derby owns some wonderful specimens, and is very interested and keen. On more than one occasion he has owed his life to his dogs. Osmaston Daisy, and Osmaston Grip have taken more poachers between them than any other dog living.' Commenting on the tracking abilities of the breed he writes: 'I was baffled to find out whence they got their speed and wonderful noses, as neither the Bulldog nor the Mastiff could be looked upon as very fast dogs or of

Sir E. Landseer's drawing of a Bulldog (1820). This was the type of animal used in the production of night dogs and in the early mastiff crosses, and bears little resemblance to today's show bulldog.

'Dogs Fighting' by George Morland (from an engraving in the Author's collection dated 1801). The winner in this battle could easily be a bullmastiff as we know it today, and bears out the author's theory that dogs of this type have existed for generations.

possessing wonderful scent. Personally I think at times the strain of blood-hound has been introduced, and that the old fashioned bulldog was used and not the modern dog'.

He summarises his article thus: 'I hope I shall have interested many who will look into the claims of a dog that is not only all British, but combines wonderful pluck and endurance with the gentleness of a lamb, and whose only aim is, if necessary to be allowed to take its death serving its master or mistress. One cannot buy devotion, but the next best thing to it is to buy a Bull-Mastiff'.

Mr J. H. Biggs mentioned above by Count Hollander was breeding Bull-Mastiffs as far back as 1908. Mr J. H. Barrowcliffe who later became the President of The Midland Bull-Mastiff Club was breeding Bull-Mastiffs during the first world war and remained active in the breed until his death. Another important figure in the breed was Mr W. Burton of Thorneywood Kennels, Nottingham, an expert breeder and trainer of 'night dogs'. His best known dog, the brindled Thorneywood Terror was supposed to have been the most perfectly trained night dog of the era. He was exhibited at the old Westminster Aquarium where he took part in fighting and downing any man prepared to take him on as a wager. Terror was always muzzled in these combats, but apparently never failed to down his man. He also gave an exhibition of his

Pre-registration bullmastiff – Osmaston Turk. Weight 120lb. The dam 'Old Nell' was half bloodhound and half mastiff.

abilities before representatives of the War Office, but I can find no evidence of this body taking the breed into its service. For those interested in Mr Burton's training methods, an article of his is printed in Barton's *Sporting Dogs – their points and management*. It is obvious from the article (1905) that the dogs were a very tough lot. Certainly the early show Bullmastiff was not an animal to be trifled with as it was very sharp, a fact not surprising when one considers the background and the use for which these dogs were bred.

In 1924 the Kennel Club gave official recognition to the breed. In the December issue of the Kennel Gazette it was reported that the Committee had decided to prepare to open a section among 'Any Other Variety' registrations for Bull-Mastiffs if pure bred as such, and when sufficient had been registered, the breed would be eligible for a place in the Register of Breeds. This announcement clarified those animals eligible as 'most important to observe the distinction between a Bull-Mastiff pure bred, and a Bull-Mastiff cross bred, the former being a dog bred with both parents and the preceeding three generations all Bull-Mastiffs without the introduction of a Mastiff or Bulldog. The term Bull-Mastiff cross bred implies the existence of a definite cross which has not yet been bred out according to Regulation 128 of the Regulations for Registration'.

With this official recognition a breed club was formed and registered at the Kennel Club on 23 June 1925. This was The Midland Bull-Mastiff Club. In

Pre-registration bullmastiff – Thorneywood Terror – a typical gamekeeper's night dog.

This is the cage in which Thorneywood Terror toured the country.

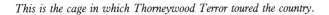

September of that year, the Midland Club drew up its rudimentary breed standard as follows:

Head
To be square and compact, on no account to be long or the Great Dane type. Muzzle to be square. Head and fairly short neck to be set on fairly well set up shoulders. Ears on no account to be large and drooping, but rather to be the size between the Bulldog and the Mastiff showing an alert expression when the dog is excited or roused. Eye to be preferably dark, although a hazel eye must not be considered a bar provided that the dog conforms to type. Slight haw not altogether detremental. An under shot mouth not a bar in view of the fact of the dog's breeding. Wrinkle on the skull desirable but not essential.

Body
Chest to be muscular and broad. Body to be well ribbed up and not too long. Even proportions to be aimed at. Dogs must not be leggy. Legs must be straight. Tendency to cow hocks or bowed front to be avoided. Tail must be thick at the top, gradually tapering, but not too fine as in the case of the Bull Terrier. Gay tail carriage a decided drawback. A cranked tail is not to be a bar although the eventual type might be improved by having a straight tail. The Bulldog type of cranked tail is bound to appear from time to time. Coat must be hard and short, similar in texture to the Mastiff or Bulldog. A shaggy coat is a decided disqualification.

Colour Etc.
To be fawn or brindle. Any shade of fawn or brindle permissible. Black masks preferable. Slight white marking on chest or toes not to be a detrement, but patches of white on body to be avoided. Breeders to remember that a dog with a poor body and a good head is quite as bad as one with a poor head and a good body.

General Features
To be aimed at in the make up of a Bull-Mastiff should be courage, activity and strength. The dog's disposition should be cheerful, and shyness the very first thing to be avoided. Intelligence must always be kept in view. This type of dog is naturally intelligent, and by careful breeding and training such intelligence can be developed very strongly.

Size
Bitches 75–90 pounds weight. Height at shoulder 23–25 inches. Dogs 90–110 pounds weight. Height at shoulder 24–26 inches. The big upstanding type of dog is to avoided. Breeders to remember that they are not to aim at producing a dog as big as a Mastiff.

On 4 January 1926 a second club was registered at the Kennel Club. This was 'The National Bullmastiff Police Dog Club', the driving force behind this

Farcroft Fidelity, born 1921.

organisation being Mr S. E. Moseley of Burslem, Staff. Mr Moseley who had been breeding Bull-Mastiffs for some years became the most important breeder of the era, in fact, if one traced the pedigrees of any bullmastiff alive today, it is absolutely certain that one would find Farcroft Fidelity as one of the ancestors, such was the importance of the Farcroft Kennels.

Before looking at Mr Moseley the man, and his dogs, I quote his formula for the production of his conception of the Bull-Mastiff.

> Taking a Mastiff bitch and a Bulldog I produce a 50/50. A bitch of these I mate to a Mastiff dog and gave me a 75 per cent Mastiff 25 per cent Bull bitch, which I mate to a 50/50 dog. A bitch from this litter is 62 1/2 per cent Mastiff 37 1/2 per cent Bulldog. I mate this to a 50/50 dog, and a bitch from this litter I put to a 62 1/2 per cent Mastiff 37 1/2 Bulldog which gives me approximately my ideal 60 per cent Mastiff 40 per cent Bulldog. I repeat this from other bloodlines as an outcross and thus I established my Farcroft strain and the Bull-Mastiff a standard breed of set type which breeds true-like produces like. This is fixing a type not merely breeding a cross bred.

Mr Moseley was basically a smallholder who kept, and bred dogs. He owned and bred Cocker Spaniels and Mastiffs, in fact in 1926 was advertising mastiff puppies for sale, and the mastiff Farcroft Watchman at stud. He had been breeding Bull-Mastiffs for some years using the prefix 'Hamil' for some, and not registering others. He was sufficiently astute to see the breed's potential as a guard dog, and the venture must have been quite lucrative during these early years. His dog Farcroft Fidelity was the first Bull-Mastiff as such to win a first prize at a show. The first show scheduling the breed was Bagnall on 19 August 1925. Fidelity was the first Bull-Mastiff to qualify for the Kennel Club's stud book, in fact Mr Moseley always claimed that Fidelity retired from the show ring unbeaten, and I find no evidence to refute this claim.

Mr Moseley's motto was 'Farcrofts are what Bull-Mastiffs should be – Faithful and Fearless but not Ferocious. Big enough to be powerful but not too big to be active'.

It was to Mr Moseley that the honour of making up the first Bull-Mastiff champion fell. His brindled bitch Farcroft Silvo who was by Hamil Grip out of Farcroft Belltong won her first CC at Crufts 1928 followed by similar successes at Manchester, the Kennel Club Show and Birmingham of the same year. This bitch won fourteen CCs in her show career and died in 1933.

If Silvo was of undisputed bullmastiff type, such a description could not have truthfully applied to Farcroft Fidelity. The late Vic Smith, who knew the dog well, said that he was agile, but long caste, had poor ear carriage and was very weak in the muzzle. Fidelity's sire, Shireland Vindictive was a brindle owned by Mr C. Pierce, a London veterinary surgeon interested in guard dogs. I believe that Shireland Vindictive excelled as a guard.

Mr Moseley continued to breed and export bullmastiffs for a number of years and whilst he may have had his critics, his rigid principles of breeding

Farcroft Tracker and litter, 1924.

Farcroft Fidelity. The first bullmastiff, as such, ever to win a first prize (1925), and a foundation sire. The owner felt that this photograph showed the 'excellent hind-quarters' which (I quote) 'would not disgrace an Alsatian'.

only from dogs of bulldog and mastiff parentage and the eradication of St Bernard and Dane crosses, paid dividends. He wrote and published a little booklet (basically to advertise his stud dogs) which he called *The Bull Mastiff, History, Standard Type and Utility.* Stud dogs were illustrated, their fees ranging from three to five guineas, and claims were made that all puppies sold were raised under ideal conditions. In actual fact, Mr Moseley had quite a team of bitches out on breeding terms, and by using his own stud dogs would buy the puppies back in for resale. Under this system a greater number of puppies could be bred than would have been possible had all brood bitches been home based, as accomodation was not very extensive.

The influence of Farcroft was great, as Mr Moseley was really the pioneer in the bullmastiff field.

In the early 1920s a man who was to hold the strongest hand in bullmastiffs during its history to date entered the ranks of the breed. This was Cyril Leeke. Like so many young men of his age, he had returned from the war to his Worcestershire farm home only to find the farming industry in a state of slump. He had enjoyed a distinguished flying career during the war and was awarded the DFC, an honour which his natural modesty made little of. As work on the farm was not possible, and not having been trained for life in any other capacity, he became a sales representative and remained in that occupation for a number of years. The work was never particularly congenial to him and with some disappointments in his personal life things looked for him (and many like him) very different from the brave new Britain of the war propaganda.

He once recounted to me how he was having lunch at a public house, and feeling generally in low spirits, when he heard the deep bark of a dog at the rear of the premises. That sound touched off something inside him. He asked the landlord what the dog was and from whom it had been obtained. It was of course a bullmastiff, and had been purchased from Mr Moseley. Cyril Leeke decided there and then that he must have a dog like it.

In 1924 he purchased a bitch from Mr Moseley reputed to be by Farcroft Staunch which was registered by Mr Leeke as Countess Sylvia. It was a purchase which he regretted as the animal was not very satisfactory, but as the urge to own a good one was still strong he purchased a puppy from a Potteries dog dealer which he registered as Sheila. It was about this time that he decided to start a bullmastiff breeding programme and took Mrs Hill as a partner in the venture. The breed captivated him and like many new recruits Mr Leeke wanted a distinctive prefix under which to register what he instinctively knew to be Sheila's progeny. He apparently puzzled for days on all sorts of names then quite suddenly realised that the shortest, simplest, and most apt was a shortened version of the breed's name so the prefix Bulmas came into being. Mated to Ch. Peter of the Fenns, Sheila produced a litter which contained Ch. Wendy of Bulmas. Wendy mated to Ch. Roger of the Fenns produced Ch. Beppo of Bulmas who passed into the ownership of Mr and Mrs J. Higginson and won a total of twenty-two CCs in his career. Ch. Beppo was a tremendous influence on the breed and helped to establish the changed head type which was to become typically Bulmas.

Mr and Mrs Higginson's introduction to bullmastiff ownership came in 1928

Old-type bulldog bred by Mr C. Derwent. It was this type of animal used in bullmastiff foundations, such as 'Wellington Marquis' – see pedigree of Ch. Roger of the Fenns in Appendix.

'Derby Grip', a pre-registration bullmastiff, in 1923.

with the purchase of an eight weeks old puppy from Jack Mason who at that time owned a well-known dog called Filbert Supreme. The puppy was bred by Rev. Pinchbeck and sired by Patrick of Crosshills out of a Fenns bitch. She was shown as Pride of Stanfell, but her winnings were not extensive as although very good-headed, she had a crank tail.

The Higginsons' next purchase was from Mr Toney, who at this time had a select kennel based on Farcroft stock. This bitch was Jessica of the Fenns who by Ch. Beppo produced amongst others Ch. Beppica of Bulmas and Bits of Stanfell (by Navigation Lion). Bits of Stanfell mated to Ch. Beppo of Bulmas produced the bitch who was to become Britain's first post-war champion bitch, Ch. Beauty of Stanfell. Beauty's sister, Bonnie of Stanfell mated to Beefy of Bulmas produced in 1944 the fawn dog whose importance in the evolution of the breed is inestimable, Ch. Branch of Bulmas.

Mr Higginson is well known as a judge and both he and Mrs Higginson have officiated in that capacity at leading shows in the country. The strength of Mr Higginson's judging, and breeding, was in the insistence on good strong head qualities and the elimination of the weak muzzled Dane type. At the time of writing both Mr and Mrs Higginson are well and still resident in Stanfell Road, Leicester from which they adopted the world known prefix. They have retired now from bullmastiff affairs.

The pre-war era boasted other breeders of importance. Mrs D. J. Nash had a very successful kennel with the Le Tasyll prefix. During the war she combined with another breeder, Miss Rose, whose Rosland dogs were well known winners. Rosland Cedric of Le Tasyll was a good example of the combined kennels. Mrs Nash's conception of the breed was for a short-backed, cobby red based on the Springwell strain of the Richardsons. Her Ch. Springwell Major went to the De Beers in South Africa to establish that company's team of guard dogs. Trixie of Le Tasyll became the property of the film star Douglas Fairbanks.

Another pre-war figure who entered the breed almost at the same time as Mr Moseley was Victor J. Smith, who purchased his first bullmastiff in 1923. His family had long been associated with the bakery business in Worcestershire and Vic followed the profession of his father, and grandfather as a master baker. At that time country deliveries of bread accounted for much business in rural areas and it was at the house of a client who was a retired Army Captain that he first saw a pair of bullmastiffs. He remembered this first encounter many years later when visiting me and seeing a tripe hanging in a tree near the kennels. He recalled how the Captain's dogs had tripes similarly hung and how the dogs used to jump up and pull at them. Few who knew Vic in his later years would have believed that as a young man he was a competition racing cyclist and later an enthusiastic motor cyclist. He was also a very capable singer with a light baritone voice, but we must return to his bullmastiffs.

Shortly after his marriage a lady purchased the house opposite to that owned by Vic and his wife. When she moved in, to Vic's great interest she brought her bullmastiff bitch with her. One afternoon Vic noticed a hawker approach the house, and also noticed the bullmastiff who was lying down behind the open bay window, raise her head, note the stranger, and lie down again. Obviously a sale did not materialise and the man became abusive. At the first sound of a raised voice the bitch jumped through the window and rough-handled the man until called off by her owner. The result of this scene was

The first litter bred by Vic Smith. By Tiger Torus ex Princess Poppy. The puppy on the extreme right of the photograph became Ch. Tiger Prince, the first bullmastiff dog champion.

110

Tiger Torus. Sire of Ch. Tiger Prince, the first bullmastiff champion dog. Jack Barnard in his booklet, 'The all British Dog – the Bullmastiff', described Tiger Torus as 'one of the finest night dogs that ever lived'.

twofold. The hawker beat a hasty retreat, and Mr and Mrs V. J. Smith decided to have a bullmastiff.

In late spring of that year they bought a bitch puppy which they later registered as Princess Poppy. She arrived at the station in a tea chest and Mrs Smith remembered how she greeted her new owners by baring her teeth as soon as the lid was removed. Princess Poppy was of somewhat obscure breeding, and not closely related to the Farcrofts. As Poppy grew, it was decided that a mate would be needed for her. An advertisement appeared in a Midlands newspaper offering a male bullmastiff for sale and giving a Birmingham address. Vic and his wife, resplendent on motor cycle and sidecar (a Brough Superior, I believe) found the advertiser, who owned a fish and chip shop in a Birmingham back street. A price was discussed and agreed, but the owner doubted if the dog could be removed as he was extremely vicious. Mrs Smith went into the back yard, put a collar on him, got him in the sidecar whilst she rode as pillion passenger back home. This dog was Tiger Torus, a red fawn who later passed to Jack Barnard and ended his days in the Lohaire Kennels of A. P. Fraser in West Lothian. I have a letter of Jack Barnard's in which he extols the virtues of Tiger Torus as 'the best guard dog I ever owned in my life, and as good a bullmastiff as any today'.

Tiger Torus mated to Princess Poppy produced Ch. Tiger Prince the breed's first dog champion who won his first CC at Crufts in 1928.

111

Ch. Tiger Prince. Winner of the first challenge certificate offered to the breed. Crufts, 1928, also Certs. at Worcester, Manchester and Kennel Club. Such experts as Sam Crabtree, Dr. Aubrey Ireland, J. J. Holgate, H. R. Brown, etc., have said, 'He is the best' and the type to breed from. Every bullmastiff sired by him and shown have been winners, including Cert. winners, 'best in show' and winners of many 1st prizes and cups, etc. Sire of dog Cert. winner, Crufts, 1931, sire of bitch Cert. winner, Birmingham, 1930. Colour red-fawn, black mack. Stud fee £3.3 plus carr.

Until his death in 1967 Vic Smith was never without at least one bullmastiff although his activities were much reduced after a serious motor accident in 1951 which crippled him severely and made him diabetic. I have what must have been the last letter written before his death and left in his papers, with the request that it should be posted to me should he die. In this he outlined his life experiences in the breed, which was an all-consuming interest to him. Amongst the other progeny of Tiger Torus was Pridzors Belle. The prefix Pridzor was taken from the name of a wood near the Smith home. Pridzors Belle was out of a mastiff bitch called Bertha who was unregistered and from unregistered parentage. Mated back to her sire (probably to improve type) Pridzors Belle produced Pridzors Princess. This bitch was in due course mated to her close relative Ch. Tiger Prince to produce Luzlow Princess. If for no other reason Luzlow Princess will be remembered as the dam of the most important sire of pre-war bullmastiffs, Ch. Roger of the Fenns (Nov. 1929 – August 1937). He was bred by J. F. Wedgwood and purchased by Mr J. E. V. Toney of Stockton Brook, Stoke on Trent who campaigned him from 1932–35. Important as his wins may have been, it was his ability as a sire which makes him noteworthy. As you will have seen in the previous paragraph his background was very much

No. 2442

The Kennel Club

Founded 1873

Patron, His Majesty the King.

President, H.R.H. the Duke of Connaught & Strathearn, K.G. &c.

This is to Certify that the Bull Mastiff (Fawn Dog) Brindle Bitch Dog "Roger Prince" KCSB 6044 F

Owner Mr. J. Smith

Date of Birth 21 June 1925

Sire Roger Prince

Breeder Owner

Dam Princess Poppy

having qualified by winning Challenge Certificates as follow,

Show		Judge
Cruft's	Feb 8, 9, 1928	Mr. H. E. Bearn, jun.
Kennel Club	Oct 10, 11, "	Mr. H. E. Watson
Manchester,	March 20, 21, 1929	Mr. J. Barnoncliffe.

is recognised as a

Champion.

Signed and Sealed on Behalf of The Kennel Club

this Fifteenth day of June, 1929

H. Bearn Secretary.

H. McCulloch Chairman.

The first champion qualification issued for a bullmastiff dog.

113

Ch. Roger of the Fenns – see Appendix for detailed pedigree.
There is no bullmastiff in the world today which does not have Ch. Roger of the
Fenns as an ancestor. It is also highly probable that this same dog features in
post-war mastiff pedigrees (see note on probable pedigree of Templecome Taurus in
Appendix).

that of a cross-bred but it was Ch. Roger of the Fenns who sired the modern
type such as Ch. Billy of Bulmas and Ch. Beppo of Bulmas, the latter being the
bridge between the pre- and post-war bullmastiff.

If study is made of the pedigree of Ch. Roger of the Fenns given in the
appendix, it will be observed that his sire Don Juan was by Farcroft Fascist ex
Pride of Birches Head. This bitch was sired by Baldurs Best who was a
cross-bred mastiff, Penkhull Lady being the product of Stapleford Agrippa,
a pre-registration bullmastiff out of Helen who was a mastiff. We have already
met Penkhull Lady as she featured in the foundation of the late Mrs Scheerboom's mastiffs of Havengore.

It is probably an opportune point here to say that the bullmastiff of the
period tended to develop along two lines. The Midland breeders always
envisaged a stocky, bully type whereas the London fanciers were following
more closely to mastiff lines.

The Hon. Mrs Murray-Smith who lived at Kensington Gate, London was a
great breed enthusiast and excellent judge. She was the cousin of Lord

Stapleford Agrippa. The only photograph extant of this pre-registration dog. Sire pedigrees of Ch. Roger of the Fenns and mastiff Ch. Bill of Havengore.

Ch. Loki of Mulorna, taken when 22 months of age and photographed with Mrs Mullin's kennel boy. Loki sired eight British champions and five overseas champions. Mrs Mullin aimed to produce soundness and activity, combined with her conception of breed type and this she achieved to a major extent. Hers was the expression that a bullmastiff should 'look at you and through you'. It became a Mulorna hallmark, as did the superb hind angulation.

Londonderry, who at that time shared her enthusiasm for the breed. One of the most successful of her dogs was Ch. Athos who was campaigned by Miss Jane Lane, a friend of Mrs Murray-Smith. Athos sired Ch. Simba, a champion in 1932 and Simba sired Ch. Wisdom and Ch. Jeanie of Wynyard. Ch. Wisdom passed into the ownership of a Mr Lionel Edwards, and it is often stated that it was the well-known animal artist who was the new owner, but this is incorrect. The Marquis of Londonderry's dogs were housed at the Millbrook kennels of another cousin, Mr Basil Kennedy, an extremely clever handler and trainer of dogs. Basil Kennedy was later to suffer the privations of a prisoner of war camp and the bitter winters of Eastern Europe. Few who knew Mr Kennedy pre-war would have realised that this man who had considerable histrionic talent and once appeared on stage as the Spanish Ambassador to the Court of King James, resplendent in plumes, ruffles, and accompanied by two bullmastiffs, would have survived such rigours. I remember seeing him at some of the early post-war shows but his kennels were never re-established and I believe that he went back to live in Ireland.

Another kennel of importance in the pre-war era was the Mulorna Kennels of Mrs Doris Mullin. Mrs Mullin owned bulldogs and dalmatians as well as her famous bullmastiffs. Post-war she added a few very useful smooth dachshunds to her team. One remembers Doris Mullin for her lively mind and great sportsmanship, plus her readiness to be self-critical. Mulorna produced a heavy, yet active type of bullmastiff epitomised by her well known Ch. Loki of Mulorna who sired fourteen champions. Some of the critics felt that the dogs were somewhat overdone in body for their height, a tendency of which the owner was well aware. All Mulornas seemed to have that exclusive eye expression which Doris used to describe as an 'at you, and through you' look, which summed it up succinctly. Her ownership of the breed began in 1924 but her most important step forward was in the purchase of the dog Tenz from Jack Barnard. Looking at the old Mulorna names you will probably have realised that many were from famous cigarette brands of the era as Doris was almost a chain smoker. Tenz probably transmitted what was to be the Mulorna head and expression and won his three challenge certificates at three consecutive shows, gaining his title in 1934.

The deer-red stud dog Rhodian would have easily become a champion had war not prevented him being shown. He lived to a great age and although almost blind and nearly eleven years old managed to break down the kennel door of an in-season bitch and mate her. The result was a fine litter, an episode which greatly appealed to the owner's sense of humour.

Rhodian was a deep mahogany red which in some lights can look almost purple in shade. We rarely see this depth of colour in Britain nowadays, but I saw one or two at the American Bullmastiff Association Speciality Show at Ox Ridge which I judged in 1983.

In the mid 1930s Mr and Mrs E. J. Warren purchased their first bullmastiff, which was of course, a brindle. Her name was Wilma of Hartford and it was from Wilma's first litter that Mrs Warren's great favourite, Big Bill of Harbex emerged. It was the Warrens who for many years battled against prejudice and the unpopularity of the brindle colour, and to whom we owe a debt today, now

117

Rhodian (at 9½ years old) left with his 19-month-old son, Loki. Mr Paul Burden of Canada imported Pioneer, Hector and Sylvia of Mulorna as foundation stock.

that we see the colour so well established. Big Bill was born in 1935 and died at the age of nearly fourteen in 1948.

Mr and Mrs Spruce had a good team of Rodenhursts and Mr Burton's Navigations were both shown and used at stud. There were other breeders, but I think it true to say that in the short space of time between the Kennel Club's acceptance of the breed and the outbreak of the second world war, remarkable strides had been made due to the increased interest in the breed, and the good influence of the breed clubs which had come into existence.

We have already mentioned the National Bullmastiff Police Dog Club. I have one of the bronze medallions which were given by the Club to major wins at shows which they supported. A bullmastiff head is portrayed in relief, and although not exactly today's type, it is easily recognisable as a bullmastiff. At one time the Midlands had a variety of clubs including the Birmingham and District Bullmastiff Club, The Midland Bullmastiff Club and the British Bullmastiff League. This latter body was formed in 1931, and after a few years of mixed fortunes, it became the premier club as the others petered out. The Bullmastiff Association was formed in 1934, the Southern Bullmastiff Society and Training Club in 1935. After the war the Welsh Bullmastiff Society, which was later renamed the Welsh and West of England Bullmastiff Society, was formed in 1946. The original intention was to form a Welsh Branch of the Southern Bullmastiff Society, but at the inaugural meeting it was decided to form an individual Welsh Club without affiliation to any other registered Club. The Bullmastiff Society of Scotland is of comparatively recent formation.

Breed type was still very variable, not only in head types, but in overall sizes, heights and weights, some arguing that as early dogs such as Tiger Torus and Thorneywood Terror weighed approximately 90 pounds, this should be the correct weight for a bullmastiff male. In the original standard drawn up by the British Bullmastiff League, dogs at 25–27 inches at the shoulder should weigh 90–110 pounds, and bitches 24–26 inches at the shoulder should be 80–90 pounds in weight. Another interesting requirement of this standard was that the muzzle should not exceed 3 1/2 inches in length.

The early and mid thirties saw a few very well known people becoming bullmastiff owners. Captain Chris Towler, who at that time was editor of *Sporting Life* bred a litter and distributed them in a manner likely to give the breed a boost in popularity. One of the puppies was presented to HRH The Duke of Gloucester and was registered as Hussar Stingo. Lord Derby owned one, as did the champion boxer Len Harvey. Yet another litter brother was presented to Arsenal Football Club and became their mascot as 'The Gunner'. Gunner was paraded round the football ground before, and after any match. In these days of football hooliganism perhaps Gunner would have served a purpose other than that of decoration, as many bullmastiffs of this era were not exactly animals to be trifled with. It should be remembered that Farcroft Fidelity's dam, Farcroft Faithful, died in defending her owner during a poaching affray on the Yorkshire moors. I quote from a letter to Mr Moseley requesting a replacement for the bitch: '. . . the kiddies wanted her brought home, so I carried her two miles and buried her where we can see the grave of the best pal man or child could ever have. True to death . . .'.

In the USA the bullmastiff became recognised in December 1933 as the result of an application from Mr J. W. Cross Jnr, who had imported stock from Mr Moseley. In 1934 the American Kennel Club published a breed standard based on that of the British Bullmastiff League. Amongst Mr Cross's later imports was Jeanette of Brooklands who was later returned to England and became an English champion. The next major importer was Mr D. McVicar, an employee on the Rockefeller Estate in Tarrytown. Again the imports came chiefly from Mr Moseley. Mr McVicar registered stock under the prefix Pocantico, some of them registered as having John D. Rockefeller as breeder.

The outbreak of hostilities in 1939 marked a temporary reduction in all bullmastiff activities and a few kennels were disbanded, but a nucleus of stock remained in sufficient strength to blossom forth after the war ended.

When peace was declared in 1945, the bullmastiff was in a comparatively healthy state. Mention has already been made of the Bulmas and Stanfell kennels which were established pre-war. Mulorna had a strong hand, Mrs Nash's De Tasylls were well to the fore, and Mr and Mrs E. J. Warren's brindles had survived the war. Mr and Mrs L. Spruce, whose Brooklands prefix was well known pre-war, had allowed it to lapse, and were obliged to use Rodenhusrt as their post-war prefix.

There were three important stud dogs which made an impact in the post-war

Mr V. J. Smith's Pridzors Alibi. Alibi won the 'Our Dogs' dog of the year competition 1952–53. Between March 16 and November, 1953, Alibi scored 1197 points on his show-ring appearance (8 points for every first prize, 2 points for every second prize, 1 point for every third prize). Alibi ended his days with Mrs Betty Smith in Midlothian, where he sired, amongst others, Ch. Romulus of Yotmas and Remus of Yotmas.

period. Ch. Billy of Stanfell was one such dog. Born in 1943 he was by Ch. Springwell Simba out of Bessie of Stanfell. Bessie was a Ch. Beppo of Bulmas daughter, ex Bits of Stanfell. Ch. Billy was owned by Mr T. Avery at Littlemore, near Oxford. Billy sired Ch. Magician of Bablock, another outstanding specimen owned by Mr Avery, but unfortunatly a non breeder. Some of Ch. Billy's well known progeny included Ch. Radcot Classic, Ch. Bulbarrs Brutus of

Ch. Bulldozer of Bulmas enjoying a novel with his friend, Miss Lucky Moore.

Radcot, Ch. Pridzors Reward, Ch. Bruce of Radcot, Ch. Pridzors Trust and Pridzors Alibi. Vic Smith campaigned Alibi, and by winning the highest number of show winning points for any dog of any breed in the period to November 1953, Alibi became the 'Dog of the Year', winning that title and trophy sponsored by *Our Dogs*. Alibi was the product of a father to daughter mating. His dam, Pridzors Jewel, was by Ch. Billy of Stanfell out of Radcot Enterprise. Two more Pridzor champions from Ch. Billy of Stanfell were Ch. Pridzors Ideal and Ch. Pridzors Trust.

It may be of interest to some that the whorls which one still occasionally sees in the bullmastiff coat, often on one and sometimes on both shoulders, usually indicates that Ch. Billy of Stanfell is an ancestor. He often produced this characteristic, which was probably inherited from his sire Ch. Springwell Simba.

Bulmas was developing not only numerically, but in stabilising the type. In the early post-war period C. R. Leeke moved to Hampton in Arden and Mrs Mary Barker took charge of the kennels. Ch. Branch of Bulmas (Beefy of Bulmas ex Bonnie of Stanfell) was extensively used at stud and produced a

C. Leeke assessing some of his young stock at Springfield Towers in 1950.

whole string of champions including Ch. Bulldozer of Bulmas, Ch. Branchella of Bulmas, Ch. Bulmas Maid Marion of Wyvernhay, Ch. Battle Royal of Bulmas, Ch. Major of Stanfell, Ch. Bimbi of Bulmas, Ch. Barnacle Bill of Bulmas, Ch. Blue Print of Bulmas and Ch. Friar Tuck in the USA.

Space at Hampton in Arden was somewhat limited for the scale of development then taking place, and almost by accident Mary Barker discovered an interesting nineteenth century 'folly' called Springfield Towers near Coleshill, Birmingham, which became the next Bulmas home.

The Bulmas strain was not faultless; light eyes bedevilled it, and mouths were not always good, but Bulmas brought the breed a huge step forward towards the now accepted breed type. Ch. Beppagain of Bulmas was exported to Mr Lee Twitty in the USA.

From Springfield Towers the kennels moved to Elmdon Park, Birmingham and with his brilliant handling, Cyril Leeke became almost invincible in the show ring. I once asked him if he would give a talk on bullmastiff handling, but he replied that it was impossible as there were no hard and fast rules and the approach to each dog is often quite different. When a dog was ready for campaigning in the show ring, it became a house dog and very much a pet and companion, and all the while its personality and temperament were being studied, and developed. All were shown on a long loose lead and the dogs rarely took their eyes off their owner/handler. Somehow, Cyril Leeke managed to get the dog looking exactly right at the precise moment that the judge was about to make his decision. There was always complete liason between owner and exhibit, and I never once saw a dog which was unhappy in his company.

The last Bulmas champion was the bitch Ch. Beauty of Bulmas who took the CC at Crufts in 1957. This was the year which saw the exodus of Bulmas from Britain to the USA when Mr Leeke accepted employment from Mr Lee Twitty who owned, and had successfully shown, some Bulmas dogs at that time. For a variety of reasons the USA venture was not a success and in 1960 Cyril Leeke and Mary Barker returned to England without any dogs, but shortly after the return Mary became Mrs C. R. Leeke.

After judging bullmastiffs at Crufts in 1963, a disillusioned and ailing Cyril Leeke cut himself off from the breed which he had helped to develop and with which he was so long associated. I managed to persuade him to attend a few bullmastiff rallies which he appeared to enjoy, but he said that he was finished with the dog game even if he still loved the dogs. He died in 1971.

As Bulmas faded in Britain, Buttonoak was developing, and partly on Bulmas lines. As is so often the case the whole thing snowballed after Mr and Mrs Terry had puchased a bullmastiff as a guard companion. The show began to interest the Terrys and so Bimbi of Bulmas was purchased from C. R. Leeke (Ch. Branch of Bulmas ex Bronzy of Bulmas). Here was a spectacular show career, and in 1951 she won Crufts, Blackpool, Brighton and Altrincham championship shows. Mated to Bulmas Marco of Lisvane, she produced a fine fawn of unmistakably Bulmas type – Antony of Buttonoak, later to become a well known champion.

Having established this very Bulmas type in the kennels Mr and Mrs Terry introduced a new bloodline in Swatchway Amethyst of Buttonoak. Amethyst

'Bulmas leaves for the USA, 1957.' Cyril Leeke (extreme left) and Mrs Mary Barker (third from left) en route plus dogs. The last Bulmas champion, Ch. Beauty of Bulmas, 2nd dog on left.

who in due course became a champion had a slightly overshot mouth, but also developed a vaginal hyperplasia which was surgically corrected. This allowed her to be mated, and by Ch. Rodenhurst Masterpiece she produced the puppy who was later to have a profound influence on the breed. That pup was Ambassador of Buttonoak born 30 May 1953.

Ambassador was flashy, a good red colour, but very different in head, body and general conformation from the somewhat more 'cloddy' Ch. Antony. He was an all rounders' choice, as what he may have lacked in true bullmastiff type, he amply compensated for in verve and showmanship. This great showmanship helped him to make bullmastiff history by winning the Gundog and Non-Sporting Group at Crufts in 1956. He was extensively used at stud both in his home kennel and to outside bitches, and his son Ch. Ambassadorson of Buttonoak followed his father's show successes. Ambassador's grandson Ch. Alaric of Buttonoak won best in show at the City of Birmingham Championship Show at Handsworth Park in 1958.

The extensive use of the Ambassador line brought an overall, if gradual change in bullmastiff type from the heavier Bulmas/Stanfell to something with a clean cut outline, probably a little more elegance, and a thinner if flashier coat. It was unfortunate that Ch. Antony of Buttonoak did not have the stud opportunities of his kennel mate. He was a fertile and keen stud but tended to panic whenever he felt that he was about to tie with a bitch. This was probably due to a difficult mating in which he may have injured himself in some way, and is another reason why I have always advocated a controlled mating in the big breeds rather than leaving the mating animals to fend for themselves. Antony ended his days with Mr and Mrs R. E. Short, but he was still apprehensive as a stud dog and was of course an older dog by then. Had Antony sired more puppies I am sure that the breed would have materially benefitted.

Mrs Mullin had a small team of stud dogs, including the now quite aged Rhodian, but the main force was his son Ch. Loki of Mulorna. Loki sired the champions St David of Gwydyr, Grantirk Griffin, Buddy of Hickathrift, Duchess of Stanfell, Tilly of Marlemac, Westgarth Black Magic, Sally Ann of Tipdixon, Christina of Brixwood and six overseas champions. In Canada, Mr Paul Burden of Fredericton imported and made up Pioneer of Mulorna, Hector of Mulorna and Sylvia of Mulorna. These dogs were housed in Paul Burdon's kennels in New Brunswick, and their owner was a very well known air ace. Apparently most of his bullmastiffs were lost in a disastrous kennel fire, after which bullmastiff breeding was abandoned.

The 1950s saw increased activity from the smaller kennels. In Wales, Mrs Storm's Taffside kennels had a run of success producing the champions Taffside Tarquin and Taffside Trina sired by Ch. Pridzors Reward. Mesdames Millard and Eaton whose kennels were strongly based on Bulmas produced some useful winners. The Misses Goodhall from Stockport developed their Goodstock kennels and produced some very good headed ones, their first champion being Ch. Goodstock Lord Joyful whose name is still seen on a few pedigrees. Mr and Mrs Higginson still bred the occasional litter, but their crowning achievement was when a home bred Ch. Bambi of Stanfell went best in show at Leicester Championship Show in 1959.

Mrs L. Matthews bred Ch. Bulbarrs Brutus, yet another development of the Ch. Billy of Stanfell line. The dam of Brutus was Bulways Bubbles, bred by Messrs W. and J. Mitchell from Cardiff. Messrs Mitchell and Mr and Mrs Storm were the backbone of the breed in the Principality, and it was their ardent campaigning of the breed at all the small Welsh shows which brought many recruits to the breed within the Principality.

The Bullturn dogs of Mrs F. Turnbull were noted winners of the era. The strain was another based on Ch. Billy of Stanfell, via his son Prince of Purbeckdine. Ch. Buoyant of Bullturn was a big winner as was Ch. Bouncer of Bullturn.

Mr and Mrs E. J. Warren still battled on with the brindles. The war had left the colour in a parlous state. Big Bill of Harbex was too old to be used at stud and was one of the few of this colour known in Britain at this stage. Mr and Mrs Warren located a son of Big Bill called Highland Laddie who was not young, and had never been used at stud. With great effort, and equal luck, Highland Laddie mated and produced the two litter brothers Peregrine and Pearly King of Harbex. Peregrine was the first brindled male to win a challenge certificate. He did this under C. R. Leeke at LKA in 1948. Pearly King lived an active life to the age of eleven, but his grandsire Big Bill was just a few months short of fourteen years of age when he died.

It was to Harbex that the honour of making up the first brindled dog

Ch. Bimbi of Bulmas. A bitch of outstanding quality which became the foundation of the famous Buttonoak Kennels of Mr and Mrs E. L. Terry.

Ch. Antony of Buttonoak, son of Ch. Bimbi of Bulmas, sired by Bulmas Marco of Lisvane.

Mr and Mrs E. J. Warren's Big Bill of Harbex (1835–1949). He won 109 awards in his show career and every brindle in the world today looks back to this dog.

Mr and Mrs E. J. Warren's Ch. Chips of Harbes, born 1949. Ch. Chips was the first brindled champion dog in the breed. Ch. Chips appeared in several films and was a great favourite at the old Pinewood Studios.

champion fell. This was Ch. Chips of Harbex, a son of Pearly King. Chips was also a well known film star and appeared in several roles in British films. One of his roles was in a film on the life of Pasteur, where he appeared as a 'savage slavering dog'. His terrifying slaver was the make up artist's skilful use of shaving soap to give the horrifying appearance. The cameras had to be careful not to film the wagging tail of Chips as he did his act. He always remembered his dressing room at the film studios and was very much the spoilt darling of the actors and stage staff.

Although never numerically large, a kennel which had a deep impact on the breed was the Bulstaff establishment of Mr and Mrs R. E. Short of Caterham. Quite apart from their dogs, Mr and Mrs Short will long be remembered as the never tiring Secretary and Treasurer of the Southern Bullmastiff Society, positions which they held for nearly twenty years. Ruth Short's first introduction to the breed was during the war when a bullmastiff was obtained as guard for her and the young family. Post-war this dog was replaced by a bitch called Tess of Halebridge obtained through the good offices of Mrs Dorothy Nash. It was from Tess that the first Bulstaff litter was bred. It included Bulstaff Gulliver, who stimulated an interest in the show ring. A whole series of bullmastiffs were bred at Caterham and helped to establish the breed in many parts of the world. Ch. Bulstaff Jolly Roger went to South Africa, Bulstaff Lavinia to Australia, Ch. (American) Bulstaff Brunhilde to the USA, where Ch. Bulstaff Tycoon also carried the flag for Caterham. Bulstaff

Veronica went to Mme Corteys in France and Bulstaff Bonne-Chance to Denmark. In later years there were exports to Holland, Bermuda, Italy, Germany, Sweden, Singapore and Thailand.

A fine dog with excellent temperament was Ch. Bulstaff Brobdingnag, a son of Ch. Ambassador of Buttonoak, and owned by Mrs Kay Burt. Barney, as he was affectionately called, was quite as expert in the obedience ring as he was in the show ring – not a usual combination for a bullmastiff.

Although a great dog in his own right, Ch. Bulstaff Brobdingnag will go down in posterity as the sire of what was probably the best bullmastiff produced by Bulstaff. This was Ch. Bulstaff Achilles. His dam was by Ch. Ambassadorson of Buttonoak out of a daughter of Ch. Antony of Buttonoak and Bulstaff Felicity. Achilles epitomised true bullmastiff type, sound, balanced and quality throughout. He was of average size, clear fawn in colour with a classic head, really dark ears, and despite his great muzzle strength he had a level bite.

He was sold to a pet home who wanted a good specimen as a guard and companion, but at six months the Shorts were asked to take him back as he was too exuberant. This they did gladly, and it must have been the luckiest

Mr and Mrs R. Short's Ch. Bulstaff Achilles who dominated the show ring in the early 1960s.

USA. Dr and Mrs Van der Valk's Ch. Bullstaff Argus of Arancrag. Sire: Ch.
Bulstaff Achilles. Dam: Wyaston Lady Hamilton. Photograph taken at 20 months
(1964). Judge: Peter Knoop. Handler: Tom Gateley. This dog was extensively used
in the USA and many of today's winners trace back to him.

repurchase in bullmastiffs. Achilles went on to set a record number of CC
wins. It was a tragedy that he became infertile quite early in life, as in my
opinion he was a dog who could have contributed as much as any to the breed.

By a strange twist of fate, Bulstaff Achilles' line is still quite strong in the
USA, but comparatively little of it remains in Britain. The USA strength came
via Ch. Bulstaff Argus of Arancrag (Ch. Bulstaff Achilles ex Wyaston Lady
Hamilton). This dog, the property of Dr J. Van Der Valk, was extensively and
successfully used in the States. Mrs Mary Prescott carried out a close breeding
programme using him as the mainstay. Mr and Mrs Pfenninger of Milford,
New Jersey, also took up the line some years ago, and are now reaping the
benefit of the continued programme. The breeder of Argus was Mrs L. Dunn,
who purchased the dam from me whilst she and her husband were temporarily
resident in Britain.

A disastrous fire at the kennels in 1951 was a set back to the Shorts, but
Ralph Short's untimely death in 1974 meant the running down of the kennels
and its ultimate demise.

There are few who can claim to having bred a champion and the dam of two
champions in their first litter. Mrs J. James, then resident in Cardiff, achieved

this, and her Ch. Morejoy Pride Amanda went on to win the bitch CC at Crufts in 1964. She was by Wyaston Captain Cuttle ex Lass of Cleobury. From a sister of Amanda came Ch. Trina of Ty-Fynnon, and Ch. Morejoy Eastern Princess who had the distinction of a group win at a championship show.

The famous Oldwell kennels of Mr H. Colliass had expanded apace during this period. An early purchase by Mr Colliass was Benign of Bulmas, who produced a litter by Peregrine of Harbex. Two of these youngsters called Taurus and Pinder appeared at Thame Show in 1947. The first of the numerous Oldwell champions was Ch. Bambino who won the bitch CC and best of breed at Crufts in 1960. Those carrying the prefix Oldwell to hit the headlines were the litter sisters Dancer and Duchess. Dancer won her third CC at Crufts in 1966. Important stud dogs followed at Oldwell. Ch. Oldwell Mi Trooper of Marbette sired the two bitch champions mentioned above, Ch. Oldwell Toby of Studbergh was used a good deal as was Ch. Dandini Prince of Oldwell; in fact the popularity of the Oldwells is such that there are few, if any bullmastiffs in Britain today which do not carry Oldwell somewhere in the pedigree.

Mrs Margaret Reynolds had by this time established her small Yorkist kennel; in fact the prefixes Yorkist and Oldwell were both granted by the Kennel Club in 1959. The first litter by a Mulorna dog (Vagabond of Mulorna) gave Mrs Reynolds her foundation dog Golden Vesta. From the line came such

Bullmastiff USA – Dr and Mrs van der Valk's Ch. Bullstaff Argus of Arancrag. Taken when 18 months of age.

Mr and Mrs Millett's homebred American and Canadian Ch. Milletts Argus on Red Titan. One of the USA's big winners, born 1964. Won his American championship points after eight shows. This photograph was used for the 1972 visualisations of the dog standards. Sire of five champions, he was in the first litter sired in the USA by Ch. Bulstaff Argus of Arancrag and was the first to defeat his sire in 'best of breed' competition.

dogs as Ch. Yorkist Magician of Oldwell, Ch. Yorkist Minstrel, Ch. Yorkist Maid Marion, Ch. Yorkist Miss Muffet, Ch. Yorkist Marquis. Yorkist Martin, a good strong dog which I always admired, won two CCs and two reserve CCs and went best in show at Thame in 1962. Yorkist Miss Meryl took part in the television filming of *The Brontes of Haworth* where she played the part of Emily's faithful dog Keeper. No one is quite sure of the exact breeding of the Bronte's dog, some thinking him 'a vast bulldog', others 'something between a bulldog and a mastiff', but Meryl played her part beautifully, but uncomfortably realistic scenes were enacted. What the producer wanted was for the dog to lie by the side of the dead mistress, but Meryl decided that this was insufficient and proceded to lie out full length on top of the 'dead' mistress and to lick her face. It was good for the drama and the viewers but as the actress said afterwards 'I nearly *did* expire with that weight across my chest'.

Mrs D. Price's Lombardy bullmastiffs were making their presence felt in the 1960s. Ch. Harvester of Lombardy became a big winner, and the sire of many successful ones. The kennel has long been associated with a good clear red colour, though of very recent times we have seen brindles being shown under the Lombardy flag. Lombardy Sonsy of Marmoss was a great headed dog and wonderful colour, whilst such stock as Ch. Tristram of Lombardy,

132

The author's Wyaston Captain Cuttle wearing antique war dog's collar.

Mrs Betty Smith (judge) with her two CC winners. Mrs J. James, Ch. Morejoy Eastern Princess. Mr A. C. Clark with Ch. Wyaston Tudor Prince.

Mr H. Colliass's Ch. Oldwell Toby of Studbergh. Sire: Ch. Master Brandy of Marbette. Dam: Miss Polly of Marbette. Extensively used at stud as was his son, Ch. Regent of Oldwell.

Mr H. Colliass's first champion, Ch. Bambino. Sire: Ace of Buttonoak. Dam: Mayqueen of Marbette.

Mr H. Colliass's Ch. Thorfin of Oldwell.

Mr. H. Colliass's Ch. Doomwatch Gipsy of Oldwell.

Mr. H. Colliass s Ch. Barnaby of Oldwell. Winner of Crufts, 1984.

Oldwell Corrallian, born 1983. Owners: Mr and Mrs P. A. Brittle. Corrallian is not only a CC winner but sire of champion Cadenham Ben Gunn, winner of two CCs at under two years of age.

Mrs D. M. Price's Ch. Harvester of Lombardy. An impressive square-skulled red, who was a big winner in the late 60s.

Mrs D. M. Price's Ch. Lombardy Tristram (1971), Sire: Ch. Lombardy Simon of Silverfarm Fortun of Lombardy.

Ch. Lombardy Llewellyn (1975) by Ch. Lombardy Tristram
Lombardy Hermia
The Lombardy Kennels have been supporters of the red colour in bullmastiffs.
Exports from Lombardy have influenced breed development in the USA and on the
continent.

Ch. Lombardy Simon of Silverfarm and Ch. Harvey of Lombardy, have truly brought the kennels to the fore. Lombardy features in many pedigrees in the USA.

Mr and Mrs W. F. Pratt's Kelwall dogs, which were originally founded on the Ch. Ambassador of Buttonoak line, have evolved as the great exponents of the brindle colouring. The most famous Kelwall, Ch. Darrell, had the distinction of winning best in show at an all-breeds championship show – a rare achievement for a bullmastiff.

Speaking of brindles, another loyal adherent to the colour when its popularity was extremely low was Mrs L. N. Parkes, who loyally showed brindles for a number of years. Her brindled stud dog Copper of Silverfarm was a great

Mrs J. Clark's Ch. Kwintra Tammy of Ty-Fynnon. Breeder: F. P. Pesticcio.

Mrs J. Clark's Ch. Wyaston Tudor Prince, bred by author. Sire: Wyaston Captain Cuttle. Dam: Wyaston Tudor Lass. This photograph shows the correct depth of brisket and overall substance which many lack today.

favourite at shows, always impeccably behaved, and obviously devoted to his owner.

Mrs J. Clark's Kwintra bullmastiffs left their mark. Her Ch. Kwintra Tammy of Ty-Fynnon was a big winner, but I think that Mrs Clark's favourite was Ch. Wyaston Tudor Prince who will always be remembered by his owner as a model of bullmastiff type and size.

To bring our review up to date, we must mention the Bunsoro Kennels of Mr and Mrs W. F. Harris who have produced some outstanding dogs over the comparatively short time in which they have been in the breed. I have considered their Ch. Donna to be almost as good as any which I have seen as was the excellent, strong yet feminine Ch. Bunsoro Penny Lane. Although comparatively inactive at the present, the Bulsoro line is being carried by the Todomas bullmastiffs of Mr Massey.

Mrs Cox whose foundation stock was from Lombardy, has developed a recognisable Colom type, and has some sound plans for the future.

In the breed and still winning is Gerald Warren with his Copperfields. His experience dates back to the early post-war years, and since his marriage has been ably assisted by his wife, and now his son. Most of the dogs from this kennel have been given names of characters from the novels of Charles Dickens.

What is a pleasing sign is the recent influx of new owners, breeders and

Mr and Mrs W. F. Harris's Ch. Bunsoro Penny Lane, born 1975. Sire: Ch. Bunsoro Cloud Burst. Dam: U-Bonny Blonde of Bunsoro.

Mr and Mrs W. F. Harris's Ch. Bunsoro Donna, born 1973. Note the substance of this bitch and the strong but correctly proportioned head. Sire: Ch. Pitmans Gentleman Jim. Dam: Bunsoro Bellestar.

exhibitors. I think it a pity that these folk were not given thee benefit of seeing the breed in the 1950s and 1960s, when one had the size and substance which in my opinion many of the modern bullmastiffs lack, but herein lies the challenge. These newer exhibitors would be well advised to look back at the past and try to recoup some of the qualities which are fast disappearing.

This condensed survey is concluded by a piece of sound advice given to me by the late Doris Mullin over thirty years ago, but which is still applicable. She wrote in a letter: 'In bullmastiff breeding be guided by one basic principle. When the day comes that you leave the breed, be able to truthfully say that through your efforts you left it just a little better than you found it.'

USA. Mrs R. La Paglia handling Mr and Mrs J. Estaban Jr's Ch. Blazins Ninja Warrior, bred by Mr and Mrs La Paglia. A bullmastiff must have strength, weight, and substance. In the ideal specimen these essentials are combined with poise, presence, and elegance. Ninja Warrior combines such qualities.

9

The Bullmastiff Breed Standard and its appraisal

The Bullmastiff Breed Standard

Characteristics
The temperament of the Bullmastiff combines high spirits, reliability, activity, endurance and alertness.

General Appearance
The Bullmastiff is a powerfully built, symmetrical dog, showing great strength, but not cumbersome.

Head and Skull
The skull should be large and square when viewed from any angle, with fair wrinkle when interested, but not when in repose. The circumference of the skull may equal the height of the dog measured at the top of the shoulder; it should be broad, and deep with good cheeks. The muzzle short, the distance from the tip of the nose to the stop shall be approximately one third of the distance from the tip of nose to the centre of the occiput, broad under the eyes and nearly parallel in width to the end of the nose; blunt and cut off square, forming a right angle with the upper line of the face, and at the same time proportionate with the skull. Underjaw broad to the end. Nose broad with widely spreading nostrils when viewed from the front; flat, not pointed or turned up in profile. Flews not pendulous, and not hanging below the level of the bottom of the lower jaw. Stop definite.

Eyes
Dark or hazel, and of medium size, set aside the width of the muzzle with furrow between. Light, or yellow eyes a fault.

Ears
V shaped, or folded back, set on wide and high, level with the occiput, giving a square appearance to the skull, which is most important. They should be small and deeper in colour than the body, and the point of the ear should be level with the eye when alert. Rose ears to be penalised.

Mouth
Mouth to be level, slightly undershot allowed, but not preferred. Canine teeth large and set wide apart, other teeth strong, even and well placed. Irregularity of teeth a fault.

Neck
Well arched, moderate length, very muscular and almost equal to the skull in circumference.

Forequarters
Chest wide, deep, well set down between the forelegs, with deep brisket. Shoulders muscular, sloping and powerful, but not overloaded. Forelegs powerful and straight, well boned and set wide apart, presenting a straight front. Pasterns straight and strong.

Body
Back short and straight, giving a compact carriage, but not so short as to interfere with activity. Roach and sway backs a fault.

Hindquarters
Loins wide and muscular with fair depth of flank. Hindlegs strong and muscular with well developed second thighs, denoting power and activity, but not cumbersome. Hocks moderately bent. Cow hocks a fault.

Feet
Not large, with rounded toes, well arched (cat feet), pads hard. Splay feet a fault.

Tail
Set high, strong at the root and tapering, reaching to the hocks, carried straight or curved, but not hound fashion. Crank tails a fault.

Coat
Short and hard giving weather protection, lying flat to the body. A tendency to long, silky, or woolly coats to be penalised.

Colour
Any shade of brindle, fawn or red, but the colour to be pure and clear. A slight white marking on the chest is permissible but not desirable. Other white markings a fault. A dark muzzle is essential, toning off towards the eye, with dark markings around the eyes giving expression. Dark toenails desirable.

Weight and size
Dogs should be 25 to 27 inches at the shoulder and 110 to 130 pounds in weight. Bitches should be 24 to 26 inches at the shoulder, and 90 to 110 pounds in weight. It must be borne in mind that size must be proportionate with weight, and soundness and activity are most essential.

★Gait
The movement should indicate power and a sense of purpose. When moving straight, neither front nor hind legs should cross, or plait. The right front and left rear leg rising and falling at the same time. A firm backline unimpaired by

the powerful thrust from the hind legs should be maintained denoting a balanced and harmonious movement.

*At the time of going to press this section has not been included in the official standard, but was submitted by the Bullmastiff Breed Council with the recommendation that it is included in any revised standard.

An Appraisal of the Bullmastiff Breed Standard

Characteristics
What the standard actually describes under this heading is the ideal temperament. I think that the characteristics of the bullmastiff are those of a reliable watch dog and guard, efficient by day and extremely watchful by night. The breed should be capable of differentiating between friend or foe.

General Appearance
'Powerfully built, symmetrical, showing great strength, but not cumbersome.'

These are excellent requirements but are they being fulfilled? What do we mean by 'powerfully built'? It suggests to me heavy bone, great muscular development, broad and deep chest. One should remember that in its pre-show days the bullmastiff's task was to hit and down a man. We saw that some of the dogs were lightish in weight at 90 pounds; but a dog of this weight who was all bone and muscle would be far more formidable than one thirty pounds heavier if underexercised and overweight. In considering weight it should be borne in mind that a comparatively small amount of bone weighs far heavier than a mass of fat. Housewives will realise the truth of this when buying meat on the bone by weight. After being boned out the joint seems to weigh very little indeed.

For some years I have been concerned with the overall lightness of the breed, especially the bitches, many of which must be under, or very near to the minimum weight and height. When judging the American Bullmastiff Association's Golden Jubilee Specialty Show at Stamford, Connecticut in 1983, it was a refreshing change to see bullmastiffs well up to both size and weight and also some good level mouths with broad underjaws.

Head and skull
As with the mastiff, the bullmastiff head description is the longest in the standard: 'Large and square when viewed from every angle with fair wrinkle when interested'.

We have quite a few roundish skulls, and plenty with excessive wrinkle. If one reads the standard correctly, there is more than a suggestion that wrinkle should not be there until the dog is interested. If, as some seem to think (and this includes some well-known judges) the head should always show wrinkle surely the words 'when interested' are irrelevant. The fact that the two words are in the standard must be of significance.

147

Bullmastiff Head. Figure 1: Correct head. Figure 2: Incorrect ear positioning on the skull, and bad carriage. Figure 3: Ears too long and houndy eyes set too high in skull. Figure 4: Weak head lacking in depth of muzzle, which is also too long and gives a Great Dane appearance. Figure 5: Overwrinkled skull, too 'bulldoggy', with an obviously badly undershot lower jaw, and ear placement too low.

The muzzle to skull proportions are approximately one third of the total head length. However we may choose to gloss over the fact fanciers have 'manufactured' this head as have bulldog breeders. The tendency to a short truncated muzzle was there, but the whims of fashion dictated that we should get it shorter. The old standard gave a maximum length of 3 1/2 inches for the muzzle. The rot set in when the standard was altered to read 'not more than one third in length'. This wording suggested that to be less than one third in length was not only correct, but desirable. It was not desirable of course and I am pleased to record that it was my proposition, carried by the Welsh and West of England Bullmastiff Society, to the Kennel Club via the Bullmastiff Breed Council, that altered the wording to 'approximately one third' which gives the necessary latitude and prevents the ambiguity of the former wording.

In animal breeding it is comparatively simple to alter the length of bones. The difficulty lies in altering the volume of tissue normally covering those bones. A classic example is the 'loose stockings' effect of the front legs of the Basset Hound. Obviously here was a short-legged hound which man decided to make even shorter, but although the bones got shorter, the skin and general tissue remains that of the longer limb, so it has to hang in creases.

The same will occur if you continue to shorten the bullmastiff muzzle to excess. Not only will you get the untypical bulldog look, but end up with all the breathing difficulties and soft palate abnormalities associated with the modern bulldog. From the point of view of physiological efficiency, and we are considering a working dog who should be efficient, a muzzle slightly longer than one third is probably more efficient than one shorter than one third. What is certainly not required is either a long, narrow muzzle or the ultra-short one. Nature in her wisdom tends always to defeat Man's meddling by lengthening the head and muzzle rather than shortening it.

If the whole head is to be square the underjaw should be broad and may be slightly undershot. If the underjaw is grossly undershot and protrudes, can one have the requisite squareness when viewed from any angle? We will consider this in the appropriate section.

Eyes

Dark or hazel-light eyes are a fault. Though quite specific, one must realise that as with many other factors, a really dark brindle is at a considerable disadvantage with eye colour. A moderately dark eye on a light fawn will appear to be within the standard's requirements but the same eye in a dark brindle will look decidedly light. It is a point which judges should bear in mind, but once bred into a strain, light eyes are difficult to eradicate so should always be looked at critically.

As a further note on eyes, though I hasten to add not in the standard, is the shape and set of the eye. The eye which gives the correct 'through you' expression is a deeply set, almond shaped eye. This must have been the requisite shape for the eye of a fighting dog as the brow protected it. The full, round eye does not give the correct expression, in my opinion, and is obviously much more vulnerable to injury.

Ears

V shaped set on wide and high, level with the occiput, small and deeper in colour than the body colour, point level with the eye when alert.

Few ears nowadays are correct in colour, many being the same shade as the body colour and some even lighter. A dark coloured ear sets off the head especially if the ear is correct in shape, size and position. My personal dislike is for the ear set too high on the skull especially if badly carried. For many years I battled with the ears of my bullmastiffs as although well placed, the correct colour, and nicely carried, they were too large. The late Dr Aubrey Ireland, a well known all rounder, in a critique of one of my bitches wrote very well of her qualities but concluded his list of virtues by writing 'a pity she has ears like cabbage leaves'.

Mouth

Level, slightly undershot allowed but not preferred.

We have allowed mouths to degenerate lamentably, and many are poor in the extreme; when judging nowadays it comes as something of a surprise to be able to see both the upper and lower dentition when the lips are pulled back. Too often one sees grossly undershot and often not very broad underjaws which protrude so far as to completely obscure the dentition of the upper jaw. It is sheer nonsense to say that you cannot get a strong broad muzzle, and a level mouth. Ch. Bulstaff Achilles, whose head was a classic, had a level mouth, as have some of today's winners. Bad mouths today are so bad that the animal must have difficulty in chewing, which from any point of view must be considered to be undesirable. I am utterly opposed to fault or fetish judging where an otherwise excellent animal is unplaced because of one gross fault, but perhaps the time has now come where really bad mouth formations should be penalised in the show ring in the hope that this may effect an improvement. In an excessively undershot mouth the muzzle cannot have the desired overall squareness, in fact some when seen in profile have the layback of jaw as in the bulldog. It is utterly wrong.

Neck

Well arched, moderate length, muscular, almost equal to skull in circumference.

A well arched longish neck gives a degree of elegance which is not out of place even in an animal of powerful build. One usually finds that when a dog has such a neck the shoulders are well placed and correctly angled. Short stuffy necks frequently accompany straight shoulders.

Forequarters

Chest deep, wide, well set down between the forelegs with deep brisket.

It is not necessary to repeat here the necessity of spring of rib etc. as these are covered in the mastiff standard and are equally applicable.

Far too many bullmastiffs in Britain have absolutely no depth of brisket; in fact they seem to have the opposite, in what someone aptly described as the 'gothic window' effect. This is wrong both by the standard and the fact that such a formation diminishes the chest capacity. In the USA a few showed this tendency, but the majority possessed the required deep brisket.

The front legs should be straight and quite parallel from shoulders to feet, so that the action when moving is quite straight, which is only possible if the bones are strong and straight.

Back

Straight, short, but not so short as to interfere with activity.

I wonder how many owners have seriously considered the implications of this requirement. What happens when we start breeding for shorter and shorter backs? An ultra-short spine will lack the flexibility of one which is longer. As we shorten the spine, we may obtain a more pleasing outline from a show point of view, but what if carried to the extreme? We should be quite literally limiting the space available for the organs of the body. The effect of such a formation could be catastrophic in the bitch, with infertility and inability to carry a litter for the requisite time. I am not advocating long backs, but, as with all things do not exaggerate this, or any of the standard's requirements, especially if exaggeration leads to physiological changes which are detrimental to the animal's health and well being.

Hindquarters

Loins wide and muscular. Hind legs strong and muscular, hocks moderately bent, cow hocks a decided fault.

I have commented fully on loins in the mastiff section. In my experience the best hind movement comes from animals with a fair, but not exaggerated hind angulation and a low set hock. In other words, the space between the pastern and the point of the hock should be short. The dog drives off the hock (see section on movement) and its formation is therefore of importance. A very prevalent fault in the breed today is for the hocks to turn out when moving, and the feet to turn in giving a bandy hock appearance which is both unsound and unsightly.

Feet

Well arched, tight, cat feet. Easily achieved in this breed where most foot defects are the result of insufficient exercise on hard surfaces.

Tail

Set high, strong at the root, tapering and reaching to the hocks carried straight or curved, but not hound fashion.

Until comparatively recently many tails had minor cranks, some only detected when the tail was pulled through the hand. Crank tails are a fault, but in my opinion a minor one. On the other hand one gets the occasional tail which is screwed like the modern bulldog tail. These are unsightly and spoil the outline. Cyril Leeke used to say that unless one got a crank tail in a litter, there were no good heads amongst the puppies, and to some extent he was correct. What I deplore is the prevalent fault of exhibits raising their tails straight up at an angle of nearly 90 degrees to the spine, and proudly waving it at this ridiculous angle when on the move. 'Hound fashion', as many will know, is this 90 degree angle but with the tip turned over towards the head. However one views it, this tail carriage is wrong. The standard is in effect saying that the tail should be carried straight, i.e. the root of the tail not raised above the level of the spine, but the end of the tail may be carried in an upward curve.

Coat

Short and hard to give weather protection, any shade of brindle, fawn or red, but the colour to be pure and clear. White markings other than slight on the chest a fault, dark muzzle essential, dark markings round the eyes to give expression.

Coat textures in the breed today are as laid down by the standard, even if some tend to be too soft. White markings are minimal, but I think it is not easy to breed brindles without a trace of white on the chest or feet. White markings on a very light fawn are far more difficult to see than the same markings on a brindle. What we have far too much of are the 'two-toned' variety red in some parts and fawn, often on the belly and the insides of the legs and up across the chest. This I feel is far worse than a few white markings. Smutty colours are faults, but excusable in very young bullmastiffs, as the smut often, though not always, comes out with the adult coat.

The term 'any shade of brindle' is a little open, and could make any base colour provided that it was brindled, acceptable by the standard. If a blue brindle cropped up, it would be eligible for exhibition as the standard stands today.

Weight and Size
These are clearly laid down, but at the present time many British exhibits must be on, or below the minima quoted, which is a pity. It is so easy to lose size in any breed, but comparatively difficult to regain it.

We do not want the breed so large that it is difficult to differentiate from the mastiff, but as we have specific weights and heights clearly stated perhaps attempts should be made to breed within those specifications.

The Author's Wyaston Tudor Sonnet. Although powerfully built and very game, she had great feminity.
Photo: D. B. Oliff.

The author's Wyaston Elizabeth Tudor, by Tiberio of Wyaston ex Wyaston Belle of Flossmere. Elizabeth Tudor was a discriminating but very definite guard. She inherited, and passed on, the deep deer-red colour of her Mulorna forebears.

Bullmastiff. Mr W. Newton with his Ch. Crailylea Sir Galahad at Crufts, 1977. The author made him best of breed at this show, and he then went on to win the working group under Mr P. Whitaker (right on photo). Sir Galahad won best of breed at Crufts, 1978 and 1979. He was reserve in working group Birmingham City championship show, 1976, and winner of working group at the Three Counties championship show, 1977. Born 24.8.74. Bred by Mr and Mrs W. A. Newton. Sire: Ch. Putmans Gentleman Jim. Dam: Suttonoak Countess Charmaine.

Ch. Sharwell. Mean Mr Mustard of Pitmans. Owned by J. L. and M. L. Leeson.
A dog of correct size and splendid temperament. Bullmastiff 'Dog of the Year',
1985.

USA. Mr and Mrs Aczel's Ch. Jubilee Governor. Born in USA 1976 and bred by owners from British imports. Sire: Ch. Lombardy Athos. Dam: Lombardy Estella.

Mr and Mrs P. Aczel's Ch. Jubilee Willie's Legacy, born in USA, 1982, bred by the owners. This dog ended up with many group placements and a 'best of breed' at a speciality show.

USA. Dr J. and Mrs van der Valk's Ch. Pridzors Anton of Buttonoak. Very much Bulmas bred, this dog was originally imported into USA by Mr R. Lee Twitty but later sold to the Van der Valks. In this photograph Mrs M. E. Twitty handled, Anton, at the 1958 American Bullmastiff Association's speciality show. Anton produced only two litters for his last owners but included two champions and a five-point major winning bitch.

American champion, Scyldocga Bairn Macgregor. Sire: Scyldocga Long John Silver. Dam: Bairn Fen. Breeder: D. J. Morrice. Owner: Russell G. and Helma N. Weeks, Ivyland, PA, USA. Mcgregor sired thirteen USA champions and three champions in Canada.

Mr T. La Paglia's Ch. Blazing Bramah Bull which the author made best bullmastiff at Bucks. County Show, USA in 1986.
Photo: J. L. Ashbey.

USA. A fine head-study, by Ashbey, of Mr and Mrs J. Esteban's Ch. Blazins Ninja Warrior. A beautifully proportioned, typical head with the correct amount of wrinkle, clean eye with a bold outlook. The ears are of the correct size and exact placement called for by the breed standard.

10

Breeding, Rearing and Management

Breeding

What can be reasonably certain in the world of dogs is that today's owner of a fair quality bitch will become tomorrow's breeder, especially if the bitch has had a few modest show wins. This fact is not deprecated, but quoted as the method by which most of the important kennels have been launched.

Before briefly sketching the principles and practices of dog breeding, the most important question which every prospective breeder should ask is why this fascinating, but often expensive occupation is about to be contemplated. If it is purely for 'the bitch's good', the project is best forgotten. Some feel that a litter helps to ward off the reproductive system problems encountered in some older bitches. I have had maiden bitches who have lived a long and healthy life, whilst the odd brood bitch has developed ovarian cysts or pyometra, the very conditions which the advocates of every bitch breeding one litter are trying to avoid. The bitch could die in whelping, or post-whelping complications, which could hardly have occurred had she remained maiden.

The second question which every prospective breeder should consider is whether the bitch is of a sufficiently high standard to be suitable as a brood. There are also those whose sole interest in dog breeding is in the production of a saleable commodity, but as such persons are unlikely to be reading this book they may be ignored. On the other hand there are the few who retain all puppies bred and have an ever growing canine family, purely for the sheer pleasure of owning them. Breeders who sell puppies should have a sense of responsibility towards the breed, their clients and their own reputations as breeders. There should be a minimal standard of breeding stock and animals who do not reach this standard should not be bred from. It is quite untrue to say that a mediocre bitch mated to a champion dog will produce worthwhile pups. As we shall see later in the chapter she could just as easily produce progeny as poor as, or even worse than herself. The results from the most carefully considered breeding plans can often be disappointing, but the poorer the stock the less are the chances of producing winners capable of reproducing their own quality.

The first stage therefore is a little self-analysis for the prospective breeder. If the points outlined so far have been considered and one has the space, time and financial resources to feed the fast-growing, hungry litters (remember that they may not sell at eight weeks of age) the following ideas on dog breeding may be useful.

161

Firstly, study the pedigree. One of the pitfalls into which many of today's breeders unwittingly fall is the doubling-up of faults which, had they a better knowledge of the animals listed on the pedigree, they would have avoided at all costs. It is the penalty which one pays for having the current influx of new owners and breeders. A pedigree should mean more than just a collection of names, some of which are written in red and prefixed by the magic word 'champion'. The fact that a dog is a champion does not necessarily mean that he is, or was, a good breeding proposition. There are plenty of champions who never sired a decent pup in their stud career simply because they were genetically incapable of transmitting the very points that gave them high show honours.

A much better way is to get an overall picture of the breed by seeing what dog produced the champions and how many of the progeny in their turn bred on similar qualities. A dog who can produce winners from bitches of various bloodlines is a far better breeding proposition than one who has won multitudinous CCs but never sired anything of quality.

The Principles of Dog Breeding

Breeding falls into two basic groups. Inbreeding (the breeding together of related stock) and outcrossing (the breeding together of stock which has no close relationship). Somewhere between the two methods comes the line breeding method where breeding to one common ancestor is practised but at the same time outcross lines are introduced in what some feel to be a safety measure.

Inbreeding

This is the method used to stabilise type, and reduce breed variations. Not only will it give physical similarity, but it has every chance of giving a far more consistent genetic make up. Inbreeding cannot produce any new abnormality as the method cannot introduce any characteristic which was not already there. What it can, and will do is to expose weaknesses being carried genetically by the stock but previously masked by outcrossing. If you really wish to know what faults are being carried in your line, inbreed for a couple of generations and the mysteries will soon be uncovered. It is this which makes the average breeder avoid inbreeding, and to blame the method for the abnormalities, or faults which are produced. It is not the inbreeding which has produced the fault; the fault was already there. Inbreeding revealed it, not produced it.

What we lack today, possibly due to economic stresses, is the willingness to cull stock either by destroying it, or by disposing of it without pedigree or with a pedigree endorsement, 'not for breeding'. Nature herself inbreeds, but Nature also culls. If we take a herd of deer for instance, the stag who heads the herd has won his position by battle, and is therefore anatomically sound and physically fit. He mates his hinds, and fights off any male who attempts to usurp his position. Those of you who know the wild red deer will recall the stag's defiant 'belling' as he warns off any other male with his awe-inspiring battle cry. He will head the herd for a few years, probably mating his own daughters and will eventually be challenged and beaten by a younger stag who has followed the herd at a safe distance and is son of the now overthrown ruler. This youngster will repeat the process but there is one fundamental difference between this and our breeding of dogs. Any weaklings, or malformed progeny thrown up by the inbreeding will either die, or be killed. Nature's formula has been followed: inbreed and cull.

All too often, and in too many breeds, we have by cossetting and medication prolonged the life of animals which, if left to Nature would have died and their weakness died with them. We have bred from such animals. How often at the ringside have we seen lame dogs, or dogs of a shambling gait due to anatomical malformations which make a mockery of a working dog; yet these animals have been, and are being used in a breeding programme.

Before an inbreeding programme can be started, the animals must be of a high quality, as to inbreed from unsound, or inferior stock is courting disaster. Outcross until you get more or less what you want, then inbreed and cull. There will be a wastage in the early stages, but in the long term it will pay dividends. For the large breeds there is one aspect of inbreeding which should be mentioned. For some inexplicable reason, inbreeding tends to reduce size, although this rarely happens in the first few inbred generations. If this happens, one can then resort to line breeding. This diluted form of inbreeding with its emphasis on a common ancestor which may carry an outcross blood-

Hind Quarters. Figure 1: The correct, well-muscled hindquarters which should be the aim of every breeder. Figure 2: Cow hocks. Figure 3: Bandy hocks – a fault prevalent in some bullmastiffs and particularly noticeable when viewed from behind when the dog is moving away.

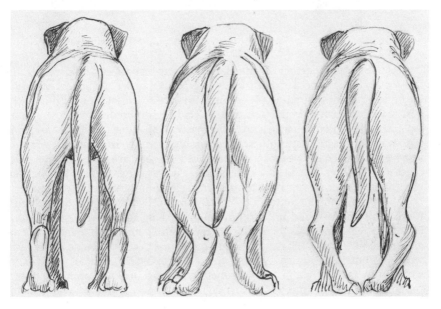

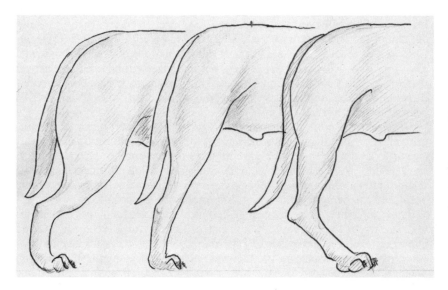

Hind Angulation. Figure 1: The correct angulation with well-turned stifle and hock. Figure 2: Narrow flank straight in stifle and hock. Figure 3: 'Sickle hock' – poor angulation and narrow flank.

line lessens the chance of establishing type and genetic purity, but can help the size question if this factor is failing.

One wit described the two methods as 'line breeding when the results are good, but inbreeding if disastrous'.

Outcrossing

This is the mating together of animals of differing bloodlines within a breed. In this method the chances of consistency of type are smaller and genetic variation far greater. In an upgrading programme it is the soundest method if only the best are retained for several generations, and then inbred.

One of the difficulties which faces the mastiff is that due to its near extinction post-war, all mastiffs are inbred; undesirable characteristics are therefore to some extent fixed and can only be reduced by selective breeding. Selective breeding, I hasten to add, does not mean mating to the reigning show champion. One cannot offset one extreme by breeding to the opposite extreme in a hope that the requisite middle line will automatically follow. It is unlikely that it will. All one will end up with are animals showing the two extremes and carrying them genetically; and unless very carefully mated, in due course they will transmit them to the next generation. Let me take two simple examples.

If in bullmastiffs one has a bitch with a long and weak muzzle, you will not correct this fault in the progeny by mating her to a dog with a muzzle of pug proportions. Your chances of correction are far greater if you mate her to a dog known to produce a high proportion of correct muzzles to bitches of varying bloodlines.

In mastiffs you will not produce the desired size by mating a small lightly boned bitch to a tall Dane type dog. If you mate such a bitch to a dog who has produced good sized stock in the past, he is far more likely to correct the fault. This is one of the reasons why I always advise prospective breeders to go to a series of dog shows and watch their breed being judged, not to see which dog the judge is giving prizes to, but to sit, catalogue in hand, and study the dogs. Read the standard, then sit and apply that knowledge to the live exhibit, and see at the same time which strain within the breed is producing the type of animal which in your opinion fits the standard. This is the first step towards successful breeding.

The whole problem lies not so much in assessing the faults which are physically manifesting themselves, but in detecting those faults carried genetically and not shown. If there are sufficient numbers of the animal's progeny being shown, there is often more than a hint of the parent's genetic make up.

Having outlined methods of breeding, one cannot continue the chapter without a section on animal genetics, a subject which seems to confuse many

Bullmastiff and Mastiff Fronts. Figure 1: Straight front with legs parallel, correct width of chest, and depth of brisket, feet pointing straight ahead. Figure 2: Unsound, bowed front, weak pasterns, out-turned feet. Figure 3: Straight front but lacking width and depth of brisket.

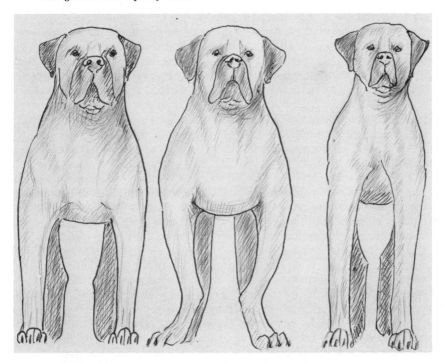

breeders. Here we will considerably simplify the mechanics of inheritance but those wishing to study the subject should read some of the specific textbooks on genetics now in print. The brief sketch given here should be sufficient to enable readers to comprehend the basic principles.

In dog breeding we deal not with two units, the stud dog, and brood bitch, but with the hundreds, or even thousands of units of inheritance called 'genes' which the sperm and ova of the two parents carry. The resultant litter will be affected, both physically, and mentally, by the manner in which these genes come together. What most breeders are seeking is the production of puppies which, with good rearing and management, will develop into show specimens. The way in which this can be guaranteed is to produce the doubly dominant or genetically pure state for those points which the breed standard demands. Such a super dog would not only be faultless himself but due to his homozygous (doubly dominant) state would pass these qualities to his offspring.

The chances of producing such a dog are pretty minimal, but it could only be achieved by a long-term inbreeding and vigorous culling in every generation until the goal was achieved. What would undoubtedly happen would be the production of a fault or weakness. Even so, the plan should be continued but it is here that temporary line breeding would help, and even where the fault occurs, violent outcrosses should not be resorted to. Use a line-bred common ancestor carrying an outcross. The whole process is a long-term one, and few would be prepared to undertake not only the expense, but the culling that would be essential. It is the only way of producing the homozygous state which is the ultimate aim in animal breeding.

Before moving on we must simply define the terms 'dominant' and 'recessive'. A dominant condition is one in which characteristics, if carried, are manifested by the dominant factor. The recessive characteristic is that which is being genetically carried but is not always physically manifest. It is often masked by the dominant. Two animals carrying the recessive factor can never produce a dominant characteristic, but two dominants carrying the recessive can, and often do, produce recessives. Such animals, although appearing dominant, are genetically impure dominant. The pure dominant, i.e. not carrying the recessive, will produce dominant, and dominant only: it is often referred to as being 'doubly dominant'.

To illustrate the gene in action, let us take the colour inheritance of mastiffs and bullmastiffs as an example. Brindle is the dominant colour of both breeds; the plain colours are recessives. It should therefore follow that a brindle to fawn mating should produce all brindles. This is rarely the case, as in both breeds most brindles are the product of brindle × plain colour and are therefore carrying the plain colour as a recessive. As we have seen earlier in the chapter, two plain colours cannot produce a brindle, and brindle, being the dominant colour, cannot be carried. Any plain colour puppy from a brindle parent will be as free from the brindle element as it would be if no brindle had ever been introduced into the breeding. To repeat the point, two fawns (or apricots) cannot produce a brindle. I recently had a fawn bitch to a young dark brindle stud dog of mine, and the resultant litter was of twelve brindles; no plain colours whatsoever were produced. The answer is that this particular dog is probably 'doubly dominant' for the brindle factor, and if so will never be able to sire anything except brindles.

In bullmastiffs brindle was for many years the cinderella colour, the reason being that often a rather old-fashioned type cropped up with a proportion of brindles. The main reason for this was the fact that Mr and Mrs Warren (Harbex) had little or no support in their struggle with the colour. Had other bullmastiff breeders been willing to take up the colour and use brindles on their more modern type bitches, the improved brindles which one sees in the show ring today would have been achieved long ago.

As another example of how genetics work, let us take the long coat factor in mastiffs. How such a coat, which is contrary to the standard, originated will never be known. It could have been carried in some of the early post-war stock as it was certainly not as common pre-war. Crusader of Sparry was actually registered as a long-coated mastiff and was used in breeding programmes. Hugh of Havengore was not perfect in coat yet sired the good-coated Ch. Dianne of Havengore and many other smooth-coated quality animals.

I am of the opinion that these long-coated mastiffs, or 'fluffies' as they are often called, inherit such a coat from a recessive gene or genes. If a smooth-coated bitch produces a long-coated puppy by a smooth-coated dog both parents are carrying the factor as a recessive. In simple Mendelian ratios, if (when adult) the apparently smooth-coated stock from the mating who are carrying the recessive are mated together, any resultant litter is likely to be 25 per cent smooth, 50 per cent smooth but carrying long-haired recessives and 25 per cent long hair. If, using the same Mendelian ratios, smooth carrying long hair is mated to long hair, the result will be 50 per cent smooth carrying long hair and 50 per cent long-haired puppies. This probably accounts for the increasing number of long-haired progeny occurring nowadays. In the past there have been matings from what appeared to be smooth coated animals, but as they were genetically impure for the factor, not only did some long coats result, but an increasing number of apparently smooth coats carried the long-coated recessive.

Dark eyes are dominant to light eyes, but I have noticed in both mastiffs and bullmastiffs that dominance is not always complete. A dark-eyed animal mated to a light eyed one does not always produce dark-eyed puppies throughout the resultant litter. The light eyes which bedevilled bullmastiffs in the early 1950s which we all thought had disappeared seem to have crept back into the breed to a minor extent thirty years later. Earlier in the chapter I mentioned that a recessive characteristic can occur many generations later when two animals carrying the recessive are mated together.

We may summarise the section (which actually requires a whole book devoted solely to the subject) as follows:

1. You will modify a fault by breeding to the opposite extreme.
2. You will do a great disservice to the breed by mating animals showing a common fault especially if it is genetically linked (i.e. inherited from a common ancestor). Long muzzles, light bones, light eyes, straight stifles, imperfect mouths, are faults which are often transmitted. Nervousness, indifferent health,

lack of size, viciousness are all characteristics which get transmitted to some degree.

3. No matter what your aim may be in breeding, it is unlikely to be achieved in the first generation. The only way to improve in quality is to outcross and cull until the envisaged type occurs, then inbreed these types and continue to rigorously cull.

The successful breeder is one who is not only prepared to admit mistakes, but who has the courage to take calculated risks, and where such risks prove unsatisfactory, not to repeat the mistake. As an old breeder of Old English Game once said to me, 'the art of breeding is not only in the knowledge of what to do, but in knowing when to stop'.

If, having read this somewhat salutory section, the reader is still prepared to breed a litter, we should consider details in breeding.

Some practical considerations

No bullmastiff, or mastiff bitch (and the same applies to the foreign mastiffs mentioned later in the book) should be bred from until at least two years of age. Much is drawn from the system during the period of tremendous growth and the laying down of the skeletal structure. A bitch in whelp before two years of age has an unnecessary taxing of her metabolism which could do untold damage to her long term well being. On the other hand the young male can be tried at stud when about ten months of age, and could be used once again when approximately eighteen months old, but in my opinion should not be given regular stud work until reaching the age of two years.

Bitches normally come on heat twice a year, the period of heat lasting about twenty-one days, during which time she is sexually attractive to the male, although she will only stand for a mating during a comparatively short time in the oestrus. Many books will say that the ideal day for mating is the thirteenth day after bleeding from the vulva was first noticed, but this is a generalisation. I have had bitches mate on the ninth day and one who would never stand for a mating until the twenty-second day and both conceived, admittedly to one of my own stud dogs.

It is presumed that the bitch owner will have selected the stud and advised the stud dog owner that the bitch is on heat. It should hardly be necessary to comment that no other dog must be given access to her. When ovulation takes place the bleeding usually disappears and the bitch shows acceptance by standing with her back braced and tail pushed to one side. She should then be ready for mating.

Many failures of conception are the result of the bitch owner's anxiety that the animal will be off heat sooner than expected: better that she is mated a little later in the oestrus than too soon. The other main cause of lack of conception is stress. All too often the bitch is taken on a long journey to the dog, pushed out of the car and expected there and then to accept an excited stud dog. She is given no time to empty bowel or bladder before being taped, held and often forced to mate. It is the complete opposite of what Nature intended. Those of us who have lived in the depths of the country for most of our lives and have had the opportunity of seeing the wild carnivores such as the fox at breeding time will realise that the vixen is pursued and played with for days by the male fox before she will allow a mating. The vixen is often coquettish and will roll about and excite him but this sex play goes on for hours, or even days. We dog breeders wish to rush everything, and it leads to failure.

Unlike most other mammals, the penis of the dog does not become fully engorged until well inside the vagina of the bitch. Once engorged it cannot be withdrawn until ejaculation is complete, and produces the effect of a pressure pump ensuring that the semen is forced forward. This is normally called 'the tie' in dog breeding circles, and many consider it to be essential to conception. It is not essential. I have known dogs who rarely if ever tied and were quite fertile. Others who have tied for as long as an hour or more produced no litter. The dog does not ejaculate semen all the while. The first ejaculate is a mild alkaline fluid, then semen is ejaculated, then more fluid. The object of the alkali is to counteract any vaginal acidity which the bitch may have.

Whilst following natural methods in most things, I am opposed to just allowing the stud dog and bitch to get on with the job of mating without supervision. Bitches often prove difficult whilst the tie is taking place and could severely injure the stud if allowed to lie down or twist over on their back, as some will attempt to do. Once the tie is established, they normally become calmer.

In more primitive times it is obvious that a male so locked in his mate was vulnerable to the attack of other males, and it is probably a defence mechanism which gives the stud dog an inclination to dismount when tied and turn himself round so that the animals are facing in opposite directions and tail to tail. I have never allowed this in any stud dog as unless assisted; it is impossible to control the two animals in this position should the necessity arise. My method is to keep the male facing in the same direction as the bitch but dismounted from her. Even with such large dogs I have controlled matings single handed by passing a lead which is on the dog's collar through the collar of the bitch. One can then draw them together if attempts are made to pull apart. Some advocate multiple matings, and in a case where the bitch has previously been difficult to get in whelp such a procedure can help, but the correct mating of two healthy animals on the appropriate day should result in conception.

After the mating is complete, the bitch should be removed and allowed to rest quietly, and the stud dog likewise, but there is a suggestion which I hope everyone will adopt.

Some of the worst fights which I have experienced here have been between kennel mates who have, as often as not been litter mates and lived peaceably together until mated. It is extremely unwise to return the stud dog after a mating to any run where he has access to other males, and the bitch should only be put back with a female kennel mate if one is sure of their reaction. It is often a help to put the mated bitch into an adjacent kennel and run until the following day when reaction can be assessed and much of the excitement died down.

Before leaving the subject of mating, I would suggest that the owner of what appears to be a non-breeding bitch has a vaginal swab taken when next the bitch is on heat. Ovulation does not follow a set pattern but when a vaginal swab is taken and a stained smear examined under the microscope, the cell structure will indicate whether or not the bitch has ovulated and is therefore ready for mating. Such a test will remove the hit and miss of the owner choosing what is presumed to be the correct day of mating.

The Gestation Period

If the diet is a good one, the bitch needs nothing different for the first five weeks after mating. It is usually about the fifth week that one can observe a thickening of the body and enlargement of the teats signifying that she is pregnant. Her diet should be rich in calcium, but not, in my opinion, on chemical calcium. Milk, cheese and yoghourt are excellent foods for the pregnant bitch, and she should have access to couch grass and other herbs which she will select for herself if given the opportunity. Exercise should never be restricted, but one should never allow a heavily in-whelp bitch to rough and tumble with her kennel mates. At the same time she should not be considered, or treated as, an invalid.

Whelping

The gestation period of sixty-three days is another arbitary calculation. A bitch carrying a large litter may whelp at any time after the fifty-eighth day. Some bitches may go on until the sixty-sixth day before they whelp, but if they go over the sixty-sixth day, I would recommend that an examination by a veterinary surgeon is carried out.

The whelping quarters should be clean, warm and well away from any disturbances and noise. The bitch should have been introduced to the whelping quarters well in advance of the actual whelping. If a whelping box is used it should be large enough to enable the bitch to lie out full length and made as free from draughts as possible, though a hothouse stuffy atmosphere should be avoided at all costs. I normally lightly tack a piece of old carpet to the bottom of the box and cover this with plenty of newspapers. Both carpet and newspapers can be easily removed after the whelping.

When whelping is imminent the bitch becomes restless, paces the room, usually begins to pant and frequently looks round at her hindquarters. She will often stretch out with her head on her paws, then sit up with her hindquarters pressed against the whelping box, and will then start to strain to produce the first puppy. As contractions become stronger the bitch usually calms down and the first puppy should be produced within half an hour of definite labour. It must be borne in mind that uterine inertia is not unknown in either breed and if no puppy is produced after half an hour of the commencement of labour a veterinary surgeonn should be called. If a bitch is to have a caesarian section for the removal of the litter, it is essential that she is not weakened and exhausted by fruitless straining. If all is well, the puppy will be born, enclosed in a membrane which the bitch will break, then bite off the umbilical chord. It is a good idea for the owner to tear the membrane from the head of the puppy if the bitch seems slow at doing this herself, and holding the puppy by the scruff of the neck give its head a shake to start it breathing. Puppies will usually then cry, which stimulates the maternal instinct of a maiden bitch, who may be confused and anxious over the whole procedure. If left to her own devices, a normal, healthy bitch will usually manage the whole operation unaided; in fact I think that the less the owner fusses, the better are the chances of a quick and easy whelping. The whelping bitch must never be just left to her own devices, as things can go wrong. All that she requires from the owner is discreet supervision.

When whelping is over let the bitch run outside to empty her bowel and bladder, and whilst doing this the soiled carpet and newspaper can be removed and replaced by clean, dry materials. When she returns place her puppies alongside her and allow her to rest and become accustomed to her maternal duties.

When breeding bullmastiffs I used an old chicken egg incubator in the whelping room. As the puppies were born and after the bitch had given them her preliminary licking I would remove them into the incubator which ran at 103°F. Not only did they dry quickly, but the all-round constant temperature proved beneficial and early post-whelping deaths negligible. I am of the opinion that much of the mortality of the newly born puppy is due to hypothermia rather than any other cause. The dry, active puppies were returned to the bitch when whelping was complete. Most bitches eat the placenta after the puppy is born and will be disinclined to eat for the first day or so after whelping. She should not be discouraged from eating the placenta as it is a perfectly natural practice, and could well have some milk-stimulating effect. She needs no bulky foods for the first few days, but copious supplies of fluids as she settles down to her nursing duties.

There is likely to be some bloody vaginal discharge for some days after whelping. This is quite normal provided that it is not copious or evil smelling. If smelly and the bitch is running a temperature a veterinary surgeon should be immediately contacted.

After the third day the bitch should be allowed out for light exercise, but one usually finds that she is disinclined to leave her litter except for short periods. Light exercise will help to tone the muscles and give an appetite. After the first few days the diet of the nursing mother should be rich in protein, with plenty of milk available for her to drink at any time, together with an unlimited supply of fresh water. Mastiffs soon foul the water with saliva when drinking, so the drinking bowl needs regular emptying and the water changed.

Many of the difficulties experienced by some breeders in bitches not producing milk is due to some extent to their frequent interference with the bitch, or puppies. If the puppies are plump-looking, quiet and lying against their dam, all is well and the whole family are best left quietly to their own devices. The more the puppies demand, the greater the stimulus for the bitch to produce milk. All that has happened is that the bitch has fulfilled her basic function in life and so there is no need for her to be perpetually hovered over, or the puppies over-handled. A strong healthy bitch should be able to rear up to eight puppies for three weeks with little or no difficulty. Supplementary feeding may be necessary if the litter is larger than this, but one should be guided by the appearance of the puppies themselves. If they start to develop a dehydrated look, especially if such a look is accompanied by a deal of crying, supplementary feeding will be necessary. At about ten days puppies begin to open their eyes but in the bullmastiff it seems to be some while before they develop the ability to focus. Should it be necessary to give supplementary feed, or hand-rear a litter the following formula has been successful whenever used:

> To half a pint raw goats milk add the beaten yolk (only) of one egg and a dessertspoonful of honey. Warm the mixture to blood heat, stirring well to ensure that the honey is dissolved. Feed at blood heat through a special feeding bottle. It is necessary to get the correct flow of milk through the teat otherwise the puppy if strong, but hungry will be over anxious and can choke if the teat hole is giving too great a flow.

The bearing of a litter of puppies is a strain on the dam and it is therefore essential that she is given a recovery time before another litter is contemplated.

Weaning

It is important that weaning is a gradual process and that the nursing bitch is allowed to feed her litter for as long as she feels inclined so to do. A good bitch will know when the demands of the whelps exceeds her milk production, and will vomit up her own food for the puppies. Again, this is a natural instinct and should not be supressed provided that the dam is not allowed to debilitate herself, or that her diet does not contain small bones which could give the pups trouble.

Weaning should commence at three weeks of age by the use of scraped raw meat. Lumps of meat are scraped with a sharp knife until pulped. Puppies smell this on the fingers and after being introduced to it will eat the pulp avidly. When this stage is reached put the meat in a shallow dish, and pour the warm milk/egg/honey mixture over it, with just enough of the fluid to cover the meat. Lapping will be quickly learnt and with this ability to lap, weaning will be well under way.

After the fourth week I give the following for bullmastiffs, double the quantities for a mastiff.

8 am: Barley kernels which have been soaked overnight in milk. These are obtainable from most health food shops and are of human consumption quality. They are a bland and highly nutritious food.
11 am: 3 ounces scraped raw meat and the weaning milk mixture.
4 pm: Cereals (or Farex) as for 8 am.
7 pm: 3 ounces pulped raw meat.

Quantities should be increased according to demand, but it is a bad practice to leave half-eaten meals lying around in the puppy quarters. Invariably the puppies tread in it, and such food encourages flies. Any food not eaten quickly should be removed, and put down later.

After the fourth week I would give one halibut liver oil capsule and a teaspoon of sterilised bone meal every other day, preferably with the meat meal.

It is a mistake to allow puppies of these heavy breeds to become too fat, yet it is essential that their diet is nutritious and ample due to the tremendous growth rate. During the first eighteen months of age, it is almost impossible to over-feed the correct protein foods. There are many who maintain that a growing mastiff needs four or five pounds of meat daily. In my opinion this is correct if red muscle meat is being fed, but if the meat is tripe, then the amounts must be considerably increased to probably six or seven pounds daily, until the animal is at least two years old when the intake can be slowly reduced. A bullmastiff puppy would need half this quantity, but the same basic principle applies. Against this, Mrs Scheerboom who never reared a weakling, told me that none of her mastiffs ever had more than two pounds of raw, red meat per day. One appreciates that Mrs Scheerboom had vast experience, and have no doubt that she was generalising in her statement. Obviously she would have been able to quickly differentiate between an adequate and inadequate diet, which someone rearing a puppy for the first time could not be expected to do.

During this long period of growth, any dog unable to select for himself the various grasses and other greenstuff necessary for health and well being should have these supplied. The feeding of minimally-washed tripe is a very useful source, as the greenstuff has already been partly digested, and whilst I feel that ox tripe feeding is excellent and the tripe may be fed raw, I would warn that

A quality 9-week-old puppy bred by Miss M. E. Perrenoud.

there is a danger of inducing worm infestation if raw sheep tripe is fed. The feeding of chemical calcium is another doubtful practice. Chemical calcium can act as a kidney irritant, and I would point out that massive overdosing of calcium and Vitamin D can have an effect on the puppy which to all intents and purposes appears to be rickets, the very condition which all the dosing was supposed to prevent. Garden quality bonemeal is not suitable, but a good sterilised bone meal is obtainable from several reliable sources. One should also remember the naturally calcium rich foods such as milk, cheese and yoghourt.

A typical daily food intake for a mastiff puppy from six months to two years would be as follows. (Bullmastiff quantities are given in brackets.)

8–9 am: 6 ounces (4 ounces) Flaked cereal soaked in milk to which an egg yolk has been added.
12 noon: 2 pounds (1 pound) raw meat cut in thin slices or-
4 pounds (2 pounds) raw ox tripe cut into strips.
5–6 pm: Repeat the 8 am feed.
8–9 pm: Repeat the 12 noon feed but add bonemeal, vitamin D as outlined in note above.

It will be noted in the diet that meat and cereal feeds are separate. This is intentional, as I feel that 'bloat' or gastric torsion is often induced by the fermentation of cereal and meat in the stomach. In all the years in which dogs alleged to be susceptible to the condition have been kept here, there has never been a case of bloat, which, in my opinion is due to this strict routine of never mixing the two foods.

Puppies should always be given large bones to gnaw and play with. They serve several purposes. Firstly they occupy the puppy's attention, and at the same time help teething. What is even more important is that the gnawing of bones is a wonderful way of making the puppy exercise his feet. If you watch a puppy bone chewing you will note that the feet are being used in many directions and for a variety of purposes – holding, scraping, flexing. All this is good natural exercise and should be encouraged. Needless to say puppies should never be given small, or splintered bones.

Some puppy rearing incidentals

Always ensure that the puppies nails are trimmed and blunt. The nails grow into small hooks and can badly lacerate the bitch's teats as the puppy paws her whilst feeding. This can be so uncomfortable for the bitch that she is dis-inclined to allow them to feed.

When the litter is about five weeks of age, the bitch should be given a raised platform where she can lie away from the demands of her ever hungry family. Clean water must always be available to her.

Treat the puppies for roundworms at an early age, and repeat as necessary. If hand-rearing has had to be resorted to, it should be remembered that in the newly-born and young pup, bowel and bladder action is produced by the bitch's licking. If hand-reared, this licking action has to be substituted by wiping the parts with cotton wool lighting soaked in olive oil. In a hand-reared litter there is a danger that the puppies in their search for food will suck the genitals of the others. This must be prevented by housing each hand-reared puppy in a sectional box.

Many breeders use infra-red heaters for puppy rearing. A dull emitter is preferable, but the actual temperature on the floor of the box should be taken. It will be found to vary considerably in differing parts of the box, and it may become necessary to use more than one lamp if the litter is large, in order to get uniformity of temperature.

Whatever form of bedding material is used for the litter, it should be easily disposable, always clean and dry. There are some excellent materials now on the market which look almost like sheepskin blankets and are not only good insulators, but apparently wash very easily.

Puppies, like humans, can get tired of the same diet and often appreciate a change; one should try to introduce variety as often as is practicable. A great appetiser for puppies is minced raw herring. Put the whole herring through the mincer and the finely ground bones will do no harm. I have always found this to be a real stimulant to waning appetites and when the herrings are in season they are reasonably priced. Puppies which are healthy are greedy feeders, but it is this very greed which necessitates supervision at feeding times. The smaller puppies can so easily be pushed out of place by the stronger litter-mates. What then happens is that either the smaller puppy loses the food or a major part of it, or gulps it ravenously, fearing that it is about to be stolen. This can have disastrous results on the digestive system, and should be avoided. Each puppy should have its own feeding dish, and if necessary the smaller, or slower feeders should be fed apart from the stronger greedy ones.

In my opinion all puppies should have as much sunlight as possible and should never be closely confined indoors. This is one of the reasons why I advocate spring litters as the puppy then has the maximum amount of sunlight at the most important stage of growth. Close confinement can make puppies shy or stupid. They should be encouraged to accept new sights, sounds and experiences, and a radio playing for an hour or two in their kennel is no bad thing.

They should not be allowed to spend too much time standing on their hind legs in an attempt to look out of their kennel, or run, especially if the puppy is heavily boned. The lightly-boned puppy is comparatively easy to rear and can commit all sorts of physical indiscretions without apparent damage, but such a pup is not the aim of the true breeder. To rear the heavily-boned puppy correctly is almost an art and it is this highly desired type which can so easily become unsound from careless rearing. A puppy at about four months of age can appear slack in shoulders, and indifferent in hind quarters but provided that one can keep excess weight off such a puppy, and it is not over-exercised, this is the type which when adult will have the desired substance and weight.

A really slow developer can be over three years of age and still not have reached physical maturity, but these are the dogs which usually stay the course and live on to a good age. There are others who look so much more mature and

175

typical at an early age and do a lot of winning as puppies because of this, but maturity does little for them. It is their early maturity which placed them ahead of their slower competitors; the latter type, however, continue to win well into middle age.

Newly born puppies usually have pink noses, although if one looks closely it is normally possible to see pigmentation in the nostril. Some inexperienced breeders have wondered if the pink nose means that the litter will all eventually have dudley noses as adults, but the pigmentation usually comes within about ten days. On the other hand I have never known the requisite black muzzle to be present in either breed on any adult unless unmistakably there whilst the puppy was in the nest. Muzzle pigmentation tends to fade rather than increase. In the mastiff, the desired black ear of the adult can be checked by looking at the edge of the ear, especially the inside edge. If a black rim of fur is present, the true black ear will be a feature of maturity.

White markings are less predictable. A white flash on the chest of a silver fawn will be hardly noticeable in the adult, but a similar marking on a brindle will look obvious indeed. One of the reasons why the brindle, which is my favourite colour, is often at a disadvantage in the show ring, is that it calls for a far more discerning appraisal than one of the plain coloured specimens. A stripe running vertically up a foreleg towards the withers can, to an inexperienced or careless judge appear to be an upright shoulder simply because the eye when assessing the exhibit is carried in this straight line. Many brindles look smaller than their plain coloured competitors when in fact they are the same size, or even larger. The colour is a natural camouflage and it is possibly for this reason that many judges find it difficult.

Choosing your puppy

It is presumed that the prospective purchaser has done the necessary homework and knows exactly what is required. It is also presumed that a reasonable breeder has been contacted and an appointment made to view the litter. To be a responsible breeder does not necessarily mean ownership of an extensive kennel, but someone whose interest goes beyond the production of a saleable commodity. I would be highly suspicious of any breeder who did not allow me to see the complete litter and also the dam of the puppies. One can get a rough idea of her size, type and temperament. After rearing a litter she is almost bound to be out of coat and not looking her best but at least one should be able to tell if she is sound, typical and healthy. If she promptly cowers, puts her tail between her legs and shoots back into her kennel, I would not entertain looking further as this temperament is so often passed on to the puppies. If on the other hand she was aggressive, I would be encouraged to look closer at her progeny. We are, after all, dealing with guard dogs, and whilst one can control and train a spirited one, you can never instil courage into a coward, and in these breeds a coward is as undesirable as it is untypical. If by chance the bitch has produced stock by a prior mating, ask to see this older stock, as it will give you some idea of the type which she is capable of producing.

Speaking quite personally, I would under no circumstances purchase a puppy produced at the interview as being the one most suitable for me, in other words chosen by the breeder for me without my being allowed to see others in the litter.

Do you wish to purchase a dog or bitch? The choice may not be yours as it is possible that a puppy of the correct sex may not be available in the litter. Dogs are larger and more impressive in these breeds than in most others: I have always said of the Molosser group that dogs and bitches are as different as the lion and lioness. Bitches are smaller, sometimes more intelligent, usually cleaner in the house, but one has the problem of the twice a year on heat period, which can be difficult especially if there is a male on the premises. Some have bitches spayed but I find this as distasteful to my concept of dog ownership as having the males castrated.

The best way to view the puppies is to have them in an outside pen to which the prospective purchaser has access. The first puppy which I would consider is the one which comes forward boldly, and with a self assured swagger. The one which I would not consider – no matter how promising from a show point of view – is the puppy which retreats back into the kennel, and never again emerges. Such a puppy rarely makes a pleasant, bold companion, and will be heavy going for any prospective purchaser.

Puppies should be adequately covered with flesh, but not fat. They should be loose-skinned, free from fleas, lice, or any evidence of skin eruptions. The following points are given as advice to any purchaser, as points which they should try to avoid. Before listing these, one should briefly look at the dilemma of the owner/breeder who may wish to retain one or possibly two of the litter, but cannot make up his or her mind on which puppy to select. Certainly the fourteen listed points are equally applicable, but the owner/breeder has (or should have) a fair indication of faults carried in the parent stock, and has an automatic advantage. What no one can accurately forecast is the ultimate size which will be obtained, which is important in large breeds. Some breeders maintain that they select when the puppies are born, and never deviate from that selection. I have always found that at about three days of age one has a better idea of the litter, but final selection is best left to six weeks. At this age, and in both breeds, the chest should be well down between the forelegs. If it isn't then it is never likely to have the requisite depth of brisket when adult. In mastiffs, if the chest comes down to about the level of the elbows at six weeks, there is every chance that the dog will end up leggy, a characteristic which is certainly not called for in the standard. Having said this, it is often quite surprising to note how puppies change and how they end up as adults. In mastiffs, bitches rarely get any taller after eighteen months of age, but they do of course, broaden and mature much later than that. Conversely mastiff dogs can grow on steadily in height after twenty months, and in many strains, the head takes up to four years to finally develop.

One should avoid the following:

1. Nervousness, in all its forms.
2. Long, silky, fluffy, or excessively woolly coats. In mastiff puppies look for 'feathering' on the tail and edges of ears, as such puppies usually grow into

excessively heavy-coated, or long-coated, adults.

3. Excessive white markings.

4. Badly cranked tails, short tails, or tails set too low, as this is often indicative of a badly set pelvis.

5. Light bone.

6. Short, stuffy neck; these often go with straight shoulders.

7. Lack of angulation in the hind limb. Also check the width of flank as too many exhibits in both breeds lack this essential.

8. Open, long or flat feet.

9. Evidence of haw (ectropion) or inturned eyelids (entropion). Excessive discharges from the eyes make one suspect entropion, or can be indicative of ill-health.

10. Badly undershot lower jaw, narrow underjaw, overshot lower jaw. In my experience badly undershot mouths in eight week old puppies tend to worsen with age, but a slightly overshot jaw can end up level. The width of underjaw is important.

11. Greenish or light blue eyes. This usually indicates that the adult will be light in the eye. Eyes should be dark brown at eight weeks, or sometimes very dark blue which turns to brown.

12. Long, thick houndy ears in either breed, or in the bullmastiff, small ears perched high on the skull appearing too close together.

13. Long, weak, pointed, or snipey muzzle, or conversely a muzzle so short as to give a bulldog or pup-like expression. Roman noses in puppies are indicative of long muzzles in adults, and one should not be taken in by the wrinkle which runs over the muzzle in a very young puppy. This wrinkle is there at that stage to accomodate the underlying bone when it elongates.

14. Lack of pigmentation, especially on the muzzle. All too often novices think that pigmentation will increase with age. The reverse is usually the case.

Having considered all these points, place the puppy on a table and look for width, and depth between the forelegs. If narrow or shallow remember that there is every possibility that this is the pattern set for the adult. Examine the spring of rib, and ensure that the ribs are rounded and well extended back. Look for good body length in the mastiff, but a more cobby and compact body in the bullmastiff.

If I were making a selection in either breed I would go for a puppy which is built like a little carthorse – broad, thick and heavily boned. I would avoid anything which is narrow, or houndy.

Of all the points, the head is the most difficult on which to make an accurate future pronouncement, and is always the last part to mature. One hears all sorts of stories of how some choose the future big winner as soon as the bitch has whelped, or at three weeks; then the head becomes plain but will eventually return to its former promise. This has not been my experience. A really exceptional head is there at birth but is never lost at any stage of growth. Every head will improve with maturity, the skull will broaden and the stop develop but I have yet to see a head which is seriously lacking stop and muzzle strength at about eight weeks develop into something exceptional. The head is of such importance in these breeds that I think a little more time spent on studying the puppy in this respect will be well rewarded.

Movement is difficult to assess in a young puppy, but look for a low set hock and a fair degree of hind angulation. These are the two factors which give drive to the hind action. I would be suspicious of any puppy which is bandy hocked (turning toes in and hocks out) or one which badly crosses its front feet when moving. Straight stifles can be seen at this stage and usually become even straighter with maturity, so the angulation question is of importance.

My final observation on choosing a puppy is to be unhurried. If, after your careful assessment on the lines outlined earlier in the chapter there are points on which you are unhappy, discuss them with someone of breed experience. Every animal has its faults. It is a question of attempting to obtain one in which faults are minimal. In the show dog I feel that the worst fault is the lack of breed type, closely followed by the fault of mediocrity, where nothing is particularly wrong with the animal, neither is there anything particularly commendable.

Buy your puppy and ensure that you obtain the pedigree, registration and any inoculation documents. Most breeders will supply you with a diet chart and my advice is that this is adhered to in the initial stages. If you decide that changes will be necessary in the diet do it gradually when the puppy has had time to settle into its new environment.

I have left probably the most important aspect of puppy rearing to this final paragraph, and that is the vexed question of exercise. Irreparable damage can occur to a young puppy taken on a lead for long walks. These breeds are intelligent and companionable and will strive to keep going even if fatigued, and probably aching in every limb. The ideal method is to have a large play area for the puppy in which it can exercise itself, then lie down and rest when tired. As it gets older, exercise can be gradually increased, and all the while the puppy needs to be taken out into situations where it meets traffic, stangers and different noises. Once adult, and built up both physically and mentally, the breeds should be capable of as much walking exercise as the owner can give, but to over-exercise a young puppy is very unwise. It is even more foolish to over-exercise if the puppy has been allowed to become overweight. In fact I will go so far as to say that overweight as puppies, in these breeds, is the cause of much sub-normal health in later life.

Some hints on show training

Much mystique surrounds the training of the successful show dog so perhaps we should look at it logically, and establish what is actually required. Basically, all that the show ring asks is to have an exhibit which can move up and down the ring, or in any direction indicated by the judge, at a normal trotting speed. It must then be capable of standing four square and looking alert whilst the judge makes his assessment. As we have already mentioned, every dog has faults, and the art of show training and presentation is for the handler to place, or move his dog so that the faults are less obvious.

There are mixed feelings on the value of dog shows. Some attach great importance to any win, at any show, and under any judge. Others put the matter into a more realistic perspective, realising that wins in poor competition are of comparatively little significance. One should also remember that an excellent dog which is poorly trained, and badly shown, will invariably be placed below one which may lack the former's quality, but has the verve, and training to show off its paces.

Before a dog is eligible for exhibition at a licensed show it must be registered at the Kennel Club, or such registration must have been applied for at the time of completing the show entry form. If the dog is registered, but in the possession of someone other than the registered owner, a registered transfer of ownership must have been made, or applied for at the Kennel Club at the time of completing the show entry form.

I would advise anyone wishing to campaign a dog at shows to first of all take ringcraft training lessons many of which are held locally. My second suggestion is that before attempting to show their dog, the prospective exhibitor spends some time at the Great Dane or Boxer rings of a championship show and make a note of the standard of handling in these breeds, so that when the time comes to exhibit, the experts can be emulated. With a few notable exceptions the handling standard in the Molosser breeds is not particularly high, but let's look at show procedure.

Firstly, the exhibit must allow itself to be handled by the judge – an indignity to any keen guard. As we said in the onset, it must move with verve and pose, or be posed when the judge is making an assessment. The next problem to which the puppy must be made accustomed is in having his mouth examined. The judge may wish to do this himself, or ask the owner to pull back the lips for the examination. I never handle mouths when judging being always conscious of the possibility of transmitting infection from one exhibit to another. Ringcraft classes will teach both exhibitor and exhibit about these necessary procedures. One should remember that the judge has a quota of work to do and does not have the time to instruct exhibitors in the art of presentation. Once in the showring it is up to you to get the most out of your exhibit, and the more practice which you give the exhibit at home, the greater your chances of success. If your dog is grovelling on the floor, or hunching his back and tucking his tail between his legs, he probably will (and should) be overlooked, but so much of the exhibit's behaviour will depend on you. In the USA most of the championship shows are a pleasure to judge as a high proportion of the exhibits are in the care of professional handlers whose incomes depend on show wins. These experts get every ounce of showmanship out of their dogs, and never take their eyes off the judge. But how do we train for the show ring?

Show training can never be started too soon, but is often difficult if left too late. From early puppyhood the future show exhibit should have been acquainted with strange sounds, smells and sights. At shows one has blaring loudspeakers, flashing cameras, the cacophony of dog noises, and the constant passing of hundreds of other dogs and their owners. Show exhibits should be conditioned from an early age into accepting these factors. This is why many breeders have a radio playing in the puppy rearing kennels as this conditions the puppy to extraneous noise.

Start show training at eight weeks by putting a light leather collar on the puppy and letting him get used to the feel of it. Many accept the collar without qualms, others try to scratch it off, but however much it is resented, leave it on all day and remove it at night. Once the collar is accepted attach a lead to it and just let the puppy drag the lead around for a few hours. It may chew the lead, or if there are two puppies together one will invariably be attracted to the other's lead and take it in the mouth for a grand game of tug-of-war. After an hour or two take the lead off, but leave the collar on. Repeat this for a few days then pick the lead up and allow the puppy to pull against it. Most will pull forward but some will try to go backwards and object. This can seriously upset the puppy and produce a phobia about leads, so if backing, and bucking, drop the lead and try again later. Once the restriction of the collar is accepted the lead battle is over and show training can commence.

Very short walks on the lead will make training easier, and if one has a good steady adult who can accompany the puppy on these walks, so much the better as the adult will give it confidence. Never use a nervous one for accompanying the pup as nervous habits are easily transmitted at this age.

You cannot begin serious show training without a thorough assessment of the puppy's temperament. A bold, boisterous puppy is comparatively easily trained as all one has to do is to channel its energy along the desired lines. If there is a tendency to shyness you must get such an animal out and about as soon as possible. As a columnist in a weekly dog paper, I regularly receive letters asking how one copes with a nervous puppy. My recommendation is that once lead training is over, one takes it along to a fairly quiet country public house as here it will often be patted and petted by customers in the bars. There have been many instances in which the recommendation has resulted in a vast improvement in the puppy's sociability, although one bullmastiff owner once told me that whilst his puppy was cured of nervousness he himself had become something of an alcoholic. Obviously a side effect of the treatment!

When you and your puppy feel happy and confident with the collar and lead, start another series of games, this time walking the pup, lead loosely in the hand, then suddenly stop, giving the order 'Stand'. On the first few occasions he will probably come to a halt with a jerk on the lead, but will soon learn that the order 'Stand' means 'Stop'. Once this lesson is over and he will halt on command, note how he adopts a natural show pose with legs well placed to evenly take the body weight. Never tire nor bore the pup, but repeat the exercise to 'stand' daily until he halts immediately the command is given. Now take the matter a stage further and get him to maintain the show stand as if in the ring, even if it is only for a few minutes, then gradually increase the standing time.

Those who saw the late Cyril Leeke piloting one of his Bulmas exhibits to the top, will remember his use of this natural show stand. Often he stood directly in front of the dog with a long, loose lead, and the exhibit oblivious to all around it except for the handler's whispered instructions. Once seen one realises how effective such a long lead, natural stance can be in the hands of an expert. The same technique was used by the late W. G. Siggers when showing his Ouborough Great Danes. Here there was complete rapport between exhibit and handler which may have appeared to be spontaneous, but was actually the result of close co-operation, and regular training.

Perhaps we do not possess the skill to bring the exhibit to this stage of show perfection so must look for an alternative. There is no alternative to lead training nor to the order to 'stand', but we can pose our dogs in a hope of showing their qualities, and, hopefully, in making their faults less obvious. In America they call this 'stacking' the dog which I find descriptive of the technique.

To very briefly describe ring procedure, the judge normally looks at each dog individually, watches it being moved, assesses it quickly, then repeats the process for the next exhibit. As he studies each one in this manner both exhibit and exhibitor should relax. Once all exhibits have been seen, and moved, the judge looks along the line to choose his winners. It is at this stage that the exhibitor should be concentrating on his exhibit, and the judge. Harking back to the USA, I find that I can normally recognise the professional handlers, not only by the expert way in which the exhibit is 'stacked', but by the fact that they look only at the exhibit, and the judge. Some of the less professional people are often looking at other exhibits, or making stance adjustments to the exhibit which are not always to its advantage. It may be difficult to maintain a show pose when one has a slow, or indecisive judge, but when the exhibit's attention is flagging a little baked liver held in the hand and just wafted under the exhibit's nose will often revive interest. Much of the expression needed in the heads of these breeds depends upon having the attention excited when the dog will lift the ears and wrinkle the brow. Some judges and exhibitors throw bunches of keys, or boxes of matches in order to attract this attention.

One can learn a great deal by watching the experts in the ring, but success will only be regularly achieved by constant practice at home. Unless you know where the faults in your exhibit lie, the necessary correction cannot be made in the ring. As an instance, a dipping topline in an exhibit can often be partly corrected by posing the dog, then giving it a slight push under the belly which will make the dog hold itself up. All too often in such a case the exhibitor stands alongside the animal and instead of posing it, will allow it to stand so slackly as to make what was a minor fault of a slight dip become one of exaggerated proportions. How often one sees a narrow fronted exhibit posed with its front legs touching. Had the legs been correctly spaced, this constructional fault would have been less apparent. Even movement can be improved, as at some speeds an indifferent mover can get along reasonably soundly. It is a question of the exhibitor knowing the pace, and adopting it every time he practices at home, or enters the show ring.

Whilst the long loose lead technique is the acme of showmanship, we can effect an alternative. The order to stand as previously outlined is the basis, but once standing a show pose can be effected by some judicious manipulation of the exhibit. Firstly, get the collar well up behind the ears, and maintain a taut lead in the right hand. With the head held up, the exhibit is less likely to want to move away. If the ear carriage is indifferent, the collar behind the ears will help to position them, also if the dog is inclined to be throaty with loose skin spoiling the outline of the neck, one can judiciously take some of this up under the collar. Now position the front legs of the exhibit by bending down and placing the left hand under the brisket and lift him just clear of the ground and gently let him down again. Invariably the front legs will be correctly positioned after such simple handling. Still maintaining a taut lead in the right hand run your left hand over the back and position the hind legs. These should be slightly drawn back, but not exaggerated otherwise the exhibit will feel uncomfortable and move the legs forward again probably at an inopportune time. By gently stroking the exhibit and repeating the order 'stand' a show pose can often be achieved provided that the lead in the right hand remains taut. Should the dog move a front leg it is not necessary to lift the complete front again but just push the elbow on the leg which has to be repositioned and the dog will move it forward.

It is very much in your own interest to ensure that on show day the dog's overall condition is one of true show bloom. Poor coat condition for instance will downgrade the exhibit, and no judge enjoys having to handle dogs with dirty, or smelly coats. Some bath the exhibits prior to the show, but there are many dry shampoos on the market which can be used if time is short. I would remind exhibitors that a dog's condition on the exterior is often indicative of its state of health within. A few raw eggs fed once or twice a week for a few weeks prior to the show will give a coat gloss and sparkle to the exhibit, as will a teaspoon of olive oil given daily on the food. These additives, plus a daily, stimulative brushing of the coat will give the all important well groomed appearance which is the hallmark of any show winner.

Many exhibitors fail to talk encouragingly to their exhibits when in the show ring. Dogs are very responsive to tones and voices, and a cheery, encouraging tone can make the world of difference to their performance. Shows should be fun both to the exhibitor and the exhibit, and one must learn to lose or win gracefully. Most judges are quite willing to discuss the merits of your exhibit after the show, but one must remember that this is just one opinion therefore one should not be too depressed by any criticisms, or elated by praise. We all hear stories of dishonesty amongst judges and reciprocal arrangements between specialist breeder judges, but whilst one cannot completely discount such stories, I think that their incidence is very minimal. What the group as a whole suffers from, are judges who are unsure of themselves and probably lacking in breed experience. Such judges usually play safely by putting up well known winners, as it calls for a degree of courage to place any exhibit over a multiple CC winner. It also calls for a high degree of breed knowledge to explain the reasons for such a placing.

Breed clubs must promote new judges, as replacements for the more senior authorities. There is a great deal to be said for the FCI system as used on the Continent, where student judges must qualify by co-judging with a number of experts, submitting a report to those experts from which it can be decided whether or not sufficient knowledge has been acquired by the student judge, or if further training and instruction is necessary.

Shows are an important shop window and should be viewed as such. They are often social occasions and a meeting place for old friends, but one should always remember that in any breed the true value to the breed lies not in what the exhibit can win but in what it begets.

Show incidentals

Show critiques are riddled with such expressions as 'needs to tighten', 'slack in shoulders', 'tendency to cow hocks', so a few short notes on how to minimise these difficulties should not come amiss.

There are many 'play exercises' which are beneficial to the general development of the musculature; so important in the giant breeds in fact I feel that many of the unsoundness difficulties suffered by the breeds are a direct result of the failure to gradually build up muscle from a comparatively early age. Give a young puppy a large shin bone to chew and see how much benefit such a bone will afford. The front feet are used to hold the bone down, the act of ripping off the flesh develops the jaw and neck muscles, also the muscles of the chest and front legs. This is one of the reasons why I am not an advocate of the modern 'all in one' diets, which may be perfectly balanced and contain all the

'Is the mastiff good with children?' is something which I am frequently asked. In this informal photograph by Mrs S. Monostori her Gwyliwr-O-Nantymynydd gives us the answer. Photo taken when mastiff was 9 months old.

elements for growth, but they remove the need for the natural exercise enjoyed by dogs, especially young dogs.

Play a gentle game of tug-of-war with the puppy giving him a length of natural hemp rope and watch the muscles being used in this simple competition. Incidentally when house training your young puppy and you find that he is gnawing furniture etc. supply him with four feet of hemp rope of about one inch diameter and encourage him to play with this. You will find that dragging this rope round the house and chewing it for jaw exercise will prevent his misdemeanours with the furniture. Poor hindquarters in puppies can often be improved out of all recognition by giving them playing exercise up sloping ground. Climbing up slopes calls for power in the hindquarters and the more the legs are sensibly used the greater the degree of muscular development. One should bear in mind that unlike the horse, all power of propulsion in the dog comes from the hind legs, the front legs doing comparatively little by comparison. The need to use the muscles on sloping ground is probably one of the reasons why in the kennels of Mr A. Davies of Nantymynydd all the inmates are particularly strong in hindquarters. This may be partly because of the owners insistence on soundness, but also to the fact that all exercising grounds are on quite steep gradients thus forcing the puppies to use, and develop their hind limbs.

The front, and chest muscles are developed by downhill exercise as are the muscles of the feet, and pasterns, as the body weight pushes the animal from behind and makes it brace itself.

Some may feel that I have overstated this play/exercise aspect of rearing, but quite apart from the physical improvements which such exercises can effect, they also help to develop a rapport between dog and owner giving both added interest.

Training to Guard

New owners frequently ask at what age the breed start to show inclination to guard. Do not expect a six months old puppy to show much determination in this sphere. In bullmastiffs I have known them to be two years of age before recognisable guarding inclinations began to show. On the other hand I recently saw a litter of mastiff puppies who at nine weeks of age barked whenever there was a strange noise outside, and stood their ground with tails erect and a true defiance.

Man work is outside the scope of this book and cannot be advised for the ordinary owner, as once a dog of this size gets out of control it can be lethal. What the average owner requires is a dog which will bark when the doorbell rings or the door is knocked. The appearance of these dogs is sufficient to deter the average wrongdoer, but at the same time I would consider it very untypical if, in an emergency, even the most docile of dogs did not react in his owners defence.

You can train a dog to bark on command by holding a favourite titbit and repeatedly saying 'bark' or 'speak'. As soon as the puppy does so, give the titbit so that the word 'bark' is associated with something pleasant, and

reaction will always be forthcoming. Once accustomed to the order get someone to knock at the door or ring the bell and again give the order 'speak'. In a
very short while the dog will begin to bark when there is a knock at the door,
which is what the average owner wants.

My Neapolitan Mastiff bitch was nine months of age when she came to me
but was then an excellent guard of the car. This inherent trait has developed
and intensified over the years, but she has received no training in what she has
to a fine art. Now at six years of age she will tolerate strangers in the house, but
very much under sufferance, and always provided that they do not attempt to
touch her. What she will not tolerate is any movement in the room should I not
be present.

She was from the time of her birth spirited, intelligent and a ringleader, but
is a dog who in the wrong hands, or if goaded, would have been capable of
homicide. It is for such reasons that details of man-work training are not given
here.

As a final note on guarding, do not dismiss as useless a dog which shows
little aggression towards strangers. Such dogs often have the ability, but
choose not to use it especially if in the company of a keen guard dog. So often
the pack tends to leave guard duties to the keen one, but once that leader goes,
one which previously seemed far too inclined to take a back seat in guarding
matters, comes right to the fore and in a surprising way. The worst guard of
the lot is the highly strung nervous animal who can be dangerous, not from
calm, determined and well thought out guarding, but from abject fear which
drives such a dog to attack purely as a means of defence. Such dogs are best
avoided.

There is merit in the test of temperament which is practised with the
Molosser breeds in Germany. The dog under test is attached to a long lead on
a running wire. With the handler out of sight, the dog is approached and
shouted at or threatened by the tester. If the dog leaps forward in an attempt to
attack it satisfies the test. It will also satisfy the test if it makes no attempt to
attack but just looks on calmly and in an unconcerned manner; it can even wag
its tail. What it must not do is to show fear or cowardice, and attempt to run
away. These are the test failures.

Far too often we overlook serious flaws in temperament in our search for
physical perfection. At the time when the mastiff was threatened with extinction
such oversights were understandable, but there are few excuses for serious
nervousness in the breed now that its numerical strength is greater worldwide
than it has been for a century. To a lesser degree the bullmastiff has its share of
nervousness, which again is totally wrong in an old guard breed.

Housing and Management of adult stock

Both the breeds seem to be more capable of tolerating dry cold than excessive
heat, and so if housed out of doors the animals should be given access to shade
in summer, and dry quarters in winter. For kennels I have always used clean
straw as bedding material as it is reasonably cheap and when the dogs have
finished with it, can be composted for the garden. Concrete runs are an

essential as they are so much easier to clean and disinfect. Some favour earth runs, but these become like a quagmire in winter, and very soon become sour and urine soaked. A concrete run also helps to keep the feet tight and the nails short.

All kennels should have ample ventilation, and a supply of clean drinking water. It is necessary to change the water at least once a day. If kennelled, all the inmates need lead exercise at least once a day, and free running exercise before being shut in for the night.

In winter I feed two meals to the adults. In the morning they have a cereals and milk meal and a feed of raw meat late in the evening and are then put back into their runs and kennels for the night. I have never fed meat or meat products with the cereals or biscuit meals. Such mixtures seem to be the frequent cause of bloat, and it cannot be completely due to good luck that during the long period of keeping the breeds I have never had a case of bloat; in fact gastric disorders are extremely rare here.

Once adult, there are several aspects of breed ownership which must be considered. For generations the progenitors of today's dogs were kept and bred as fighting and guarding breeds, so that just beneath the surface of what appears to be a highly civilised dog these old inbred elements are lying in a semi-dormant state. You cannot treat the Molosser group of breeds as you would a German Shepherd dog, for instance, although that breed is also a notable guard dog. There are exceptions, but I would consider it unwise to run two adult males together without supervision, and the same applies to a slightly lesser degree with bitches.

There have been occasions here when two bitches who have been littermates and lived together for years will, for no apparent reason, start a fight, and once having fought cannot be trusted to ever again live peaceably together. Fights are never pleasant and my advice to any owner is to do the utmost to prevent a fight occurring. Once a dog has become an inveterate fighter, life is difficult for both owner and the rest of the animals in the kennel, so always try to avoid the type of situation likely to provoke fighting. If in a public place the dog should be on a lead and therefore able to be controlled. If a fight breaks out at home the owner must act quickly as these dogs bite and hold resulting in untold damage in a very short time. I keep leather collars on the more aggressive element as this gives some anchorage point if one has to pull them away once separated from the actual battle. Once the dogs are separated one must be shut in a kennel quickly, as given a chance both will return to the fray with added vigour.

Some recommend that playing a hosepipe on the fighters will break it up, but I have never found this to be of any use. On occasion I have had some success by throwing a coat over the heads of the two assailants then pulling them apart and quickly separating. What one should also remember is that the excitement of fights is contagious, and if other dogs are free, these too will pitch in and get the whole thing out of control. It is for this reason that I never exercise more than two dogs together.

Wounds resulting from fights are invariably deep seated, and care should be taken to keep them open so that they can discharge. Bathe the wound daily with warm water to which an antiseptic has been added, but if the skin has been slashed as it sometimes is in a bad fight, a veterinary surgeon should be consulted as the wound may need to be sutured. You may be fortunate and keep these dogs for many years without an outbreak of fighting, and I maintain that the best way to stop a fight is by preventing it from starting. These are not toy breeds, and unless the owner realises that it is possible for them to react violently on occasion, he may be totally unaware and unprepared if that occasion arises. The owner must always be head of the pack and each inmate must be made to realise this, but the necessary superiority does not have to be induced by corporal punishment. As intelligent breeds they have a great desire to please their owner and it is this which every owner should exploit. If I may quote my Neapolitan mastiff as an example, this bitch, who is quite prepared to take on anything be it human or animal, becomes so distressed if I shout at her in a scolding manner that she sneaks upstairs and lies under the bed for as long as two hours and then comes warily down to test the atmosphere. If spoken to and patted, her customary self-confidence is restored, but she is filled with contrition if she realises that she has given displeasure.

Lifespan

One is often asked about the life expectancy of these breeds, and it is not easy to answer the question. So many factors come together in determining the length of life, and longevity may to some extent be genetically controlled. The oldest bullmastiff which we have ever owned lived to 14 1/2 years of age, but eight is (I suspect) the bullmastiff average. Much will depend on the feeding, exercise and whether or not the owner has allowed the animal to become grossly overweight, a condition which will certainly help to shorten life.

The average mastiff seems to be capable of living slightly longer, and from statistics which I have collected over the years nine seems to be an average age. Mrs A. Davies's Mifanwy O Nantymynydd was over fourteen when she died but the owner agrees that this was the exception rather than the rule.

When I had bullmastiffs it seemed to me that things seemed to start going wrong with them healthwise at about seven. Once clear of this critical period and into their eighth year, they went on quite happily for a few more years.

Contrary to some beliefs, old dogs need nutritious food and possibly some mineral or vitamin supplements, as in old age they seem unable to absorb and utilise their food's nutriment as they did when young. As with young puppies they should not be over-exercised, but allowed to take exactly the amount of exercise which they instinctively know to be necessary.

11

Foreign Mastiffs

This chapter briefly describes the various mastiff breeds which exist in Europe today. Some, such as the Fila Brasiliero which have been in Germany for thirty years, maintain a presence in one country but of recent times appear to be spreading throughout Europe. It cannot be proven that these breeds share a common ancestry, but those of us who have owned these foreign mastiffs often find traits and characteristics which one normally associates with the British mastiff breeds.

Some feel that there are sufficient breeds already in Britain to satisfy all needs and tastes, therefore the importation and breeding of more mastiff types is not necessary. I disagree with such sentiments as each of the foreign dogs has its own characteristics, even if the common theme of guarding runs through all of them. Many are well worthy of support, are interesting and very capable of performing the duties for which they were evolved. A condensed version of the breed standard is given, and each breed illustrated with at least one photograph of a typical specimen.

The Mastino Napoletano (Neapolitan Mastiff)

This is Italy's native mastiff which for centuries has guarded houses and property chiefly in Southern Italy and more specifically in and around Naples. As with the English breeds, fully documented history is difficult, the breed being as much a part of Naples that few records have ever been considered to be necessary. For centuries it has been valued as a guard dog par excellence, and this ability is still very much alive in the breed today.

Piero Scanziani, who did more than anyone to bring the Mastino to the notice of the show public, has stated that at the time of Pinelli (1781–1835) the breed was known in Rome as it is the subject of both paintings and sculpture by that artist. The Mastino was also modelled as small crib statuettes used during the Christmas festival for Nativity cribs. Some of the surviving statuettes are extremely old, and help to prove that not only was the breed known centuries ago, but that the basic type has not materially altered during the passage of time.

The first occasion when the breed was on public exhibition in Italy was in 1946 when eight were entered and described as 'grasp dogs'. Piero Scanziani, who had bred bulldogs and boxers saw the Mastini and fell for a steel blue male called Guaglione and unsuccessfully attempted to buy him. Like most specimens of the breed at that time, he was of unrecorded parentage. This is not

Neapolitan Mastiff: 'Artos von Starnbergsee'. Sire: Enea di Ponzano; dam: Bavaria von Vagatenhof. Owner: Frau u. Suss, Germany. This typical mastino is free from exaggeration and particularly sound both physically and in temperament. Artos has been Clubseiger on two occasions. Compare this photograph of a Mastino with cropped ears and Britain's Kwintra Herca. Ear cropping alters the expression.

surprising in a breed which for centuries has been kept as a watch and guard dog. Some time later Signor Scanziani managed to buy Guaglione and made him the first champion in the breed.

In the meanwhile he had made a thorough search of the Naples area and purchased stock of varying type, but useful in an upgrading breeding programme. At his Villanova kennels near Rome, Signor Scanziani began a breeding programme whose influence has spread throughout the world of the show Mastino. In 1963 the Società Amorati Mastini Napoletano was formed and a definitive standard drawn up and published in 1971. If Guaglione was the modern father of the breed, the black bitch Pacchiana must be considered to be the true matriarch.

Mated to Guaglione she produced, amongst others, Specs di Villanova, who mated back to her sire produced two important champions, Ursus di Villanova and Uno di Villanova. Ursus di Villanova is behind the breeding of some of the famous dogs of the Ponzano kennels of Mario Querci. The line also formed the basis of Dr Benelli's Canedoro mastini, Ch. Verone del Canedoro being a direct descendant.

Southern Italy had, and still has, not only the strong mastino tradition, but a distinct heavy, short legged type with tremendous bone, and particularly strong heads. These so called Zaccaro types were obtained by inbreeding over several generations. Perhaps soundness was not foremost in the originator's mind, but the Zaccaro with its great bone and overall weight and substance has its place in the breed. A judicious admixture of Zaccaro with the northern Italian bloodlines would probably give us the show qualities of the north with the added breadth and weight of Zaccaro.

Germany now possesses the cream of the Italian bloodlines and the admixture is a possibility. Frau L. Denger who had bred cocker spaniels for years took up the mastino cause and bred her first litter in 1976. I had the pleasure of seeing over her Colosseo Avallu kennels in 1984 and was impressed by the uniformity and temperament of its inmates. Stock from here has been sent worldwide including Britain, Spain, Switzeraland, Belgium, Texas, Florida and Mexico.

Herr Kurt Reimann of Hamburg kept a representative kennel of mastini for some years, but at the moment the kennels have been disbanded. One hopes that this is only temporary as there were few more enthusiastic owners than the Reimanns. Herr Jurgen Didion owns a collection of mastini which includes many from the Naples area. These seem to be now upgrading the breed in

Sig: Mario Querci with (left to right) Italian + FCI World champion Rebecca di Ponzano; Italian Ch. Argo di Ponzano; Italian Ch. Quintiliana di Ponzano.

Germany as some interesting progeny are being exhibited.

Italy still has some excellent kennels, and Mario Querci's Ponzano kennels have made a great contribution to the breed. The Ponzano dogs have been successfully shown internationally, and feature in many winning pedigrees.

The first pair of Mastini in Britain came in the 1970s imported by Mr T. Lewis of The Kensington Dog Bureau. The male, Kronus della Presse, was mahogany and the bitch Ursula black. After a slow breeding start Ursula produced litters by Kronus which were the foundations for Britain. Puppies of this breeding found their way to Scandinavia, and to the Reimann kennels in Germany. Kronus, mated to Lucia, a black daughter of Ursula and by Kronus, produced, among others, Rosemaund Nina and my own Rosemaund Netta. Nina passed into the ownership of Mrs Jean Clark and in due course was mated to her imported stud, Winner di Colosseo Avallu. This was the foundation of Mrs Clark's Kwintra kennels in Gloucestershire. Winner is a litter brother to Ch. Wallia.

Unlike so many of these breeds, the mastino has been the subject of at least three Italian, and one German book. Information on the breed in English is not easily obtained, although the German/English *Molosser Magazine* a bi-lingual publication, carries breed news. America seems set for some mastino publicity as Tobin Jackson of the well known Deer Run mastiff kennels has decided to take up the breed over there.

Neapolitan Mastiff: Mrs J. Clark's Kwintra Herca. As a British-bred dog the ears are not cropped.

Germany. Herr E. Alexander's Blacksmith Britta. One of Germany's leading bitches.

Characteristics
The mastino is a guard dog of large size, and majestic appearance, courageous, highly intelligent and matchless defender of owner and property. It is deeply affectionate to its owner, but needs firm, but kind handling especially when young. Maturity is rarely achieved before four years of age, and males have been known to be sexually immature until two years old.

Synopsis of breed standard
The weight range is 110–150 pounds. In the male shoulder height should be 25 1/2–28 1/1 inches at the shoulder, bitches 23 1/2–27 inches at the shoulder, with a tolerance of 3/4 inch above or below these heights.

The head is massive, with broad, short skull. The directions of the upper longitudinal axes of the skull and muzzle are parallel. The skin is abundant with wrinkles, and folds. The length of the muzzle to the total length of head is in a ratio of 2 to 1. This means that the muzzle from the tip of the nose to centre of eyes should be half the length of the distance between the eyes and the occipital crest. The lips are thick textured and heavy, the upper lips when viewed from the front should form an inverted V, the jaws well developed with scissors, or pincers bite. The eyes are set in sub frontal position, widely spaced, and fairly deep set. Eye colour is dependent on coat colour, but should be generally darker. If not cropped, the ears should be small, set on well above the zygomatic arch, and hang flat. The neck should be short, stocky and extraordinarily muscular. The lower part of the neck should have much loose skin to form a dewlap which should be neither too abundant, nor undivided. The dewlap begins at the lower jaw, and reaches to approximately the mid-point of the neck.

Long, slightly sloping, well muscled shoulders are required. The length of body should exceed the height at the withers. Feet are oval in shape with arched toes, and lean, hard pads. The chest should be broad with exceptionally well developed pectoral muscles, the rib cage wide, and descending to the level of the elbow or slightly below. The circumference of the rib cage should be approximately 1/4 more than the height at the withers. The line of the belly should be almost horizontal, the loins broad and the hollow of the flank, minimal.

The hindquarters should denote power, be well boned and covered with well defined and prominent muscles. The coat is to be dense, smooth, fine, short, but of hard texture. Colours allowed are grey, black, mouse grey, blue grey, brindle, fawn, mahogany, or deer red.

It is essential that the abundant skin which covers the body is not tightly adherent to the underlying tissue, but with loose connective tissue on all parts of the body. The tail if undocked tapers towards the tip, and in repose is carried as a sabre tail, and never straight up, or curled over the back. It should be horizontal with the backline when the dog is in action. It is normally docked two fifths of its length.

The gait of this breed is one of its characteristics and all too often mis-understood. The movement at the walk is slow, ponderous, slouching and loose jointed, rather in the manner of a bear. The trot is slow but the strides cover a lot of ground. Pacing is often observed in this breed, and has been unjustifiably penalised. Pacing is a characteristic gait of many heavy animals. The mastino when moving should maintain the level topline and produce a smooth, effortless pace in keeping with its weight and size.

In my opinion this is a guard breed which has a great deal to offer. It appears to have few inherent health problems, is adaptable, responsive and its high intelligence makes it a desirable animal. Despite the heavy bodies of this breed, their ability to move with an almost feline elasticity is remarkable, as is the tremendous arc through which the head and neck can move. This is another breed characteristic, as is the lowering of the head when moving.

I do not consider this to be a breed to be shut away, or chained without human contact. The unstinting affection which these dogs have for their owners needs an outlet. It seems to me that if deprived of the requisite object of affection, the temperament can be ruined, and viciousness is then more than possible.

Since coming to the notice of the public the breed has achieved a following in many parts of the world. I hope that with its increasing show popularity breeders will not overlook the more utilitarian aspects of the mastino which have been bred into it for centuries.

Mastin Espanol

This is sometimes called mastiff of Leon, Mastiff of Extremadura, or mastiff of La Mancha in its native Spain.

The origins of this handsome breed are not completely known, but it would appear from historical references that the breed was known in the middle ages as a guard dog for the cattle and flocks of sheep during their movement to new pastures in summer, and the return for winter. Some feel that the Velasquez portrait 'Las Meninas' in the Prado Museum shows a true Spanish mastiff, and one must agree that the type is very similar to today's specimens of the breed. As with the mastino napoletano, its entrance into the sphere of a show dog is a comparatively new role, and its first breed club was formed in 1981. Señora L. G. Sanchez Arjona, when Secretary of the breed club, told me that in her opinion there were probably fifteen thousand mastins in Spain and that the best of these would still be found with the shepherds, although nowadays the breed is being used as guard of factories, villas and military installations.

Appearance and Character
Although for centuries this breed has been associated with sheep, it is in no way a herding dog but a true Molosser of great height, girth and proportional musculature. The breed is large, the coat of medium length and the whole bearing is that of a dog which is sure and proud of itself. It is affectionate, gentle, intelligent and noble, but its considerable strength makes it a formidable guard. It is not quarrelsome with other dogs. Although noble by nature the ancient ferocity of the breed appears as soon as it sees an enemy of its master's property or stock. This characteristic is accentuated at night when the mastin

Mastin Espanol: Puppy bitch judged by the author at Nurenberg, 1985.
Photo: H. Lohmann.

will often react in an aggressive manner to persons with whom during the day he had been quite peaceful.

Description of Standard

The standard asks for a minimum height at the shoulder, but there is no maximum: males 77 cm (approximately 30 inches), females 72 cm (approximately 28 inches).

The girth to measure more than the height at the shoulder, but balance is essential both when standing and moving.

The head is large, strong, square, the occiput is marked and the width of the head must at least equal its length, the muzzle to be broad to the end. The nose is to be black, moist and with large, wide nostrils. The upper lip should amply cover the lower, the lips junctures should be loose, and the mucous membranes black. A scissors bite is required with strong teeth, the canine teeth to be large. The eyes should be small in relation to the skull, almond in shape, dark, or hazel, alert looking but gentle in expression. The eyes are capable of giving a look of great severity when confronted with strangers, the eyelids thick and black pigmented. Ears should be medium in size. The body should give the impression of unity and strength, yet remain flexible and agile. The ribs to be deep, and well sprung, the back long, wide and powerful. It is essential that the topline is horizontal to the ground both when moving, and standing, so that the dog is always of the same height at rump and withers.

The tail is strong, flexible and covered with hair which is longer than that on the rest of the body. It is carried low in repose reaching to the hocks. When excited, or moving it will be carried raised and ruffled at the end, but must never be curled, or right up over the back.

The front should be straight, strongly boned, the feet to be catlike with tight arched toes. In the hindquarters angulation should be such as to allow movement of ease, force and elegance. The hocks should be strong. A typical coat is one which is thick and semi-long, heavier over the shoulders, longer and silkier on the tail. Colours can be any shade of yellow, red, fawn or black, brindle, together with combinations of those colours such as pied.

The movement of this breed is free and powerful, especially at the trot; pacing should not be encouraged. Temperament is of utmost importance and an excessively shy, nervous dog is untypical in temperament, as is an over-aggressive animal.

Dogue de Bordeaux

This French Molosser is considered by some to be a direct descendant of the *alans* of the Middle Ages. Others suggest some mastiff or bulldog blood, as the breed has over the centuries been used as a fighting dog and as a guard of cattle against the depredations of wolves and bears.

Whilst there are no specimens in Britain at the moment, there have been various attempts to establish it here since the early importations of 1885. It is of some significance that one of the importers of that period was Mr Sam Woodiwiss, a well-known judge of mastiffs and bulldogs; in fact it was through the good offices of Mr Woodiwiss that Mrs Scheerboom purchased her original mastiff. Mr M. C. Brooke was also an importer and, seeking to establish the old fighting type, he brought over from France a fawn called Matador du Midi. This young dog was a descendant of Caporal a well known fighting dog of the Pyrenees who weighed 108 pounds and stood nearly 25 inches at the shoulder and was 26 inches round the skull.

All the French imports had cropped ears, and ear cropping in Britain continued with the British bred stock until the Kennel Club brought out its anti-cropping regulations. Apparently this so changed the appearance of the breed that interest in it fell off, and eventually the dogs owned by Mr Brooke were sold to Canada.

Some idea of the enthusiasm for the Bordeaux can be judged from the fact that a club was formed and was well supported. It was Mr Brooke who in conjunction with the French authorities drew up the breed standard much of which is in use today.

It would appear that there is now a revival of interest in the breed not only in France, but in the Netherlands, and in Germany. Some feel that a rough similarity to the bullmastiff is to the detriment of both breeds on the Continent, but on closer scrutiny it will be found that the breeds are quite different.

Although not the largest of the Molosser group, the Dogue de Bordeaux is in every way a representative member of that group. Its powerful head, body and

A particularly fine Dogue de Bordeaux. Whilst some feel that this breed is similar to the bullmastiff, the excessive skull wrinkle which the standard calls for on the Bordeaux would be untypical on a bullmastiff.

limbs, with great musculature and low-set body, is custom built for the old type of fighting dog. The head which should be ploughed with wrinkle, is large, square and expressive. In conformation the skull is short and should be at least equal in circumference to the dog's height at the shoulder. The cheeks should be well developed, the muzzle short, strong with an undershot jaw projecting at least 1/4 inch giving it an upsweep accentuated by the thick underlip. The ears should be small, slightly raised at the base and falling backwards. The stop should be definite with a deep sunken depression running up through the forehead. The eyes are widely spaced and oval shaped which, with the pronounced eyebrows combine to give the breed its characteristic expression.

The mask may be red or black. Many feel that the black mask is not as typical and suggests mastiff crossings, but both masks are acceptable in the showring. If the mask is dark it should not be as dark as in the mastiff or bullmastiff.

The typical Bordeaux body is broad, powerful and deep with well developed musculature especially in the upper arm. The circumference of the chest should be greater than the height at the shoulder. The false ribs are set well back, and the dog heavy in bone throughout especially on the front legs.

The hindquarters should be adequately angulated and although in this breed the hindquarters are of somewhat lighter build than the forequarters, the muscles throughout the hindquarters should be well pronounced, especially the muscles of the second thigh.

The tail is wide at the root, deeply set and not reaching below the hock. The height should be 58–66 cm at the shoulder, bitches may be somewhat less. The weight for dogs is a minimum of 45 kilos, and bitches 40 kilos.

The breed is affectionate to its owner, and a loyal guard whose strong bite and great body strength make it a fearless adversary.

The Fila Brasiliero

The original purpose of this breed, which was evolved in Brazil, was as a guard of slaves. If a slave attempted to break ranks, the dogs attacked, and it is this history of use as an attacking guard dog plus the fact that the breed was, and still is, used for jaguar hunting which has given the breed its natural sharpness.

It is probable that an admixture of bulldog, mastiff and bloodhound went into the evolution of the breed, plus some of the indigenous dogs. In more recent times the Fila has, in some parts of its native country, been crossed with other breeds, but due to the efforts of Dr Paulo Santos Cruz and the *Club do Aprimoramento do Fila Brasiliero* true lines are now being perpetuated.

This is not a breed to be taken up by an amateur, yet a characteristic of the Fila is its complete devotion to the owner and his immediate family, to the total exclusion of every other human being. It is therefore necessary not only to feed and house the dog correctly, but to give it the maximum contact with the owner. If the breed is too closely confined and without owner contact, not only can the temperament be ruined, but the dog become poor in condition and development.

Maturity of body and mind is rarely achieved until the Fila is three years of age but there is a need for correct and controlled training throughout this growth period. The dogs have an inherent dislike for strangers and an adulation of the owners. Aggression may not be obvious in a young puppy but as the character develops there is a gradually evolving, but distinct aggression. This makes it essential that at an early age the puppy is controlled, and taught that an attack is not called for in the presence of strangers. At the same time he should meet, and have contact with all members of the owner's household, especially if there are children, as only by doing this can the essential relationship be established.

As the young dog grows so will his aggression against everything, and it is then that the first lessons in control must be given. If one encourages the natural sharpness of the breed one could end up with an animal which cannot be taken off the owner's premises as he will attempt to attack everything even if on a lead. This is a very self-willed breed, and obedience can only be achieved by co-operation, preferably by the owner himself as trainer. Excessive force, or excessive punishment by the owner will be detrimental, as it would be offensive to the breed's basic sensitivity.

The Fila is a scenting dog but not a sporting animal, although hunting seems

Fila Braziliero. 'Magia da Carolina' owned by A. and L. Siqueira, Jr. Braganca Paulista, Brazil. This wonderful head-study shows the perfect head proportions of a typical Fila, and the correct ear placement. The Fila Brasiliero has not reached Britain as yet, but is beginning to make inroads into the USA, and is strong on the Continent, especially in Germany, where its qualities as a guard dog are appreciated.

to be a natural instinct. Because of the basic freedom enjoyed in Brazil the breed can mature mentally and physically. A characteristic of the Fila is that attack is always extremely swift, and from any position, with little or no forewarning that an attack is imminent.

Appearance
A large, strong dog of typically molossoid type, strongly boned, and of compact structure, giving the impression of power.

Character
Most of the time the Fila does not hide his aversion to strangers or love for owners and immediate family. Their devotion has become a proverb of obedience and fidelity. In consequence he is an unsurpassed guard but also capable of cattle herding and big game hunting. Outside his home and if in the presence of his owner, he should show an indifference to passers by.

Movement
Catlike, with long elastic strides. Pacing is a characteristic of the movement and when walking the head is normally carried lower than the backline. When trotting a smooth easy long reach is achieved covering a good deal of ground. The gallop is at an incredible speed for a dog of this size. Due to his articulations typical of molossoids the Fila's movements give the impression (which is borne out in fact) that the dog is capable of very rapid, and instant changes of direction.

Breed Standard
The head is big and heavy, the skull tending to be square in shape with the length of muzzle being 40 per cent of the total length of the head. The cheeks should show some wrinkle. There should be little or no stop, the skull should have a well developed occiput and in profile the stop is well defined by the eyebrows. The muzzle, which should balance the skull, should be strong, broad and of great depth.

The teeth should not be long, but very wide, and the upper cutting teeth very sharp. Scissors or pincer bite.

The large V shaped ears are set well back on the skull; implantation is in line with the upper part of the eye.

The eyes are of medium or large size almond shaped and placed well apart. Dropped lids should not be considered a fault, as it enhances the sad expression typical of the Fila. The colour of eye can be from yellow to dark brown dependent upon the coat colour.

The body should be strong with thick, loose skin, the chest well let down to at least the level of the elbows and the ribs well sprung without interfering with the position of the shoulders. The lower line of the body should be parallel to the ground and never tucked up at the belly, but following a smooth ascending line.

The tail is very broad at the base and tapering to reach the hock. When alert the tail is raised and makes a curve at the end, but must never be curled or carried over the back.

Forelegs should be straight, strongly boned and perfectly vertical from the side view and parallel from front view. The hindlegs should not be as heavily boned and with moderate angulation.

The skin should be loose and thick all over the body especially on the chest and neck where it presents a well developed dewlap. The coat is short, soft, dense and smooth.

All colours and their combinations are acceptable with the exception of entirely white dogs, but it is recommended that uniformity of marking and good pigmentation should be aimed at (approximately one third white allowed).

Height minimum 27 inches (males), minimum 24 inches (bitches).

Weight minimum 110 pounds (males), 90 pounds (bitches).

Disqualifying faults
Cropped ears, mutilated tail, flesh coloured nose, undershot jaw showing teeth when the jaw is closed, all white coat colour, monorchid or cryptorchid, blue eyes.

The Tibetan Mastiff

To end, let us look briefly at the breed which Wynn and many subsequent writers considered to be the progenitor of all the Molosser group.

Wynn's theory that the Indian or Tibetan Mastiff migrated south with the nomadic tribes, moving firstly into the Middle East, then into Eastern Europe, can neither be proved or disproved. There is ample evidence that a heavy-coated, large mastiff type dog existed in Tibet up to the early part of this century. It is pure speculation that the breed was the root stock of our present day dogs, but Marco Polo (1254–1324) remarked that in his travels in Tibet he saw dogs 'as large as asses'.

In 1800, Samuel Turner, an employee of the East India Company, went to Tibet and in a series of articles, described the people and their trading methods. In one article he wrote of how impressed he was by the sight of a herd of yaks being guarded at night by 'two large Tibetan dogs'. He described them as being 'large enough to fight a lion if the dog's courage was equalled by its size'.

HRH King Edward VII, when Prince of Wales, was interested in foreign dogs and had at least two Tibetan mastiffs imported into Britain, but both proved to be very short lived. In the present century, Major McDougall exhibited a true Tibetan mastiff called Bhoetan. The dog was shown in 1906, and awarded high prizes as the best foreign dog. Bhoetan had been obtained during the last Llasa Expedition under Sir Francis Younghusband.

Further proof of the existence of such a dog can be seen in a stuffed head of a Tibetan mastiff which is used as a mascot in the inn called *The Dog and Muffler* at Joyford, near Coleford in Gloucestershire. When I first saw this head and asked the landlord about its origin he told me that he had purchased it in a Cardiff junk shop. He had no idea what breed it was except for some indistinct writing on a piece of paper glued to the back of the wooden plinth on which the

Tibetan mastiff: 'Yi-dam Faisal-Padu', German bred and owned. This head shows much more of a Molosser type than many. Too many Tibetan mastiffs being shown today are of a decidedly Novawart type, lacking the skull breadth and the strong, truncated muzzle which the photograph shows.

head was mounted. This said that the dog was owned by an English Army doctor who had served on the Indian north-west frontier. It was acquired as a puppy, and brought back to Britain on the owners retirement when he took up residence in Monmouth. The dog lived to be fourteen years of age. It must have been an impressive animal with a longish coat with thick undercoat; the animal being a reddish brindle. Obviously the taxidermist had taken up some of the pendulous flews.

We can safely assume that such a breed existed in Tibet, but the old breed was very different from some of the lightly built, herding type Tibetans being exhibited at the present time. It could be that the old type has changed, and with the dissolution of many of the monasteries, the true breed become rare, but some feel that by breeding with the lighter herding type dog, some of the old type may crop up.

I am told that Miss Ann Roher of the USA has devoted a great deal of time in searching for, and studying the breed, and in 1970 had reached the conclusion that it was becoming extinct. However, she found, and imported, a Tibetan which was black and tan. This was St Mary's Yullha of Lantang. Another import into the USA was Jumlas Kalu of Jumla, a black male from Western Nepal. His head may not have been the old mastiff type but he seems to have had weight and substance. Germany has another import from Nepal called Tu-Bo, who has contributed to the breed in both the USA and Europe.

Having seen these Nepalese dogs, I had presumed that unless one crossed one of these types with a long haired mastiff, and evolve a breeding programme around the crosses until type was re-established, the true Tibetan mastiff was extinct. I was therefore delighted to recently receive photographs of a true mastiff type taken by two Italian explorers, Alfonso Bietolini and Gianfranco Bracci. Signor Mario Zacchi, with whom I have corresponded on the subject, has recently sent me the photographs, and article which appeared in the magazine *Natura*. The dog is depicted with a child, but was described as being fierce and of larger size than his western counterparts.

The dog was used to guard the nomadic camp whilst the menfolk took the yak herd higher in the mountains, and the altitude at the point where the photograph was taken in Tibet was five thousand metres. He is described as having a loud and raucous voice like a fog horn, and wearing a collar made of yak skin with the yak hair still intact. His heavy coat is matted but when one considers the primitive manner in which these dogs are kept, this is not surprising. The nomads' next camp was near lake Yangcho Tso and here the land rises to seven thousand metres. Fish caught in the lake are hung to dry and it is possible that the dog's diet would include dried fish and possibly yak offal.

If Wynn and his many copiers are correct in attributing all the fascinating mastiff breeds to this one common ancestor, I hope that those interested in perpetuating the breed will try to obtain something from the nomads in Tibet in order to establish true type.

Synopsis of the breed standard

Conformation
A large, powerful dog, sturdily built, with distinctive double coat and ruff round the neck and shoulders, extending to the occiput. The tail is carried

204

high over the back, is thick and heavily feathered. Males to be a minimum of 26 inches at the withers, females 24 inches.

The temperament should show courage, an aloofness with strangers, but yet a good natured family companion.

The skull is wedge-shaped, broad, flat, with a slightly sloping stop. The muzzle to be blunt, and one third of the skull's length. It should not be coarse or snipey. Ears are to be V shaped with rounded tips, the eyes small, almond shaped, and set obliquely, light to dark amber in colour.

The body should show a broad rib cage, full broad chest, and level topline. The hindquarters are powerful and well muscled, with moderate angulation. The movement should be free and vigorous, with elasticity and a smooth powerful stride. Colour may be black, sable, red or blue. Tan markings should be clearly defined on the solid colour and confined to two spots over the eyes, on the sides of the muzzle, on the throat, two spots on the chest and on the inside of the hind legs and on the forelegs from the carpus to the toes.

List of Mastiff Champions

(The date is that of the Kennel Club Stud Book recording champion status)

1960
Hotspot of Havengore. d.
Withybush Crispin. d.
Withybush Fausta. b.

1961
Olwen of Parcwood. b.

1962
Weatherhill Milf Manetta. b.

1963
nil.

1964
Balint of Havengore. d.
Rhinehart of Blackroc. d.
Withybush Oscar. d.
Dawn of Havengore. b.
Stormy Petrel of Blackroc. b.

1965
Weatherhill Thor. d.
Falcon of Blackroc. d.
Bathsheba of Kisumu. b.
Fatima of Kisumu. b.
Weatherhill Milf Manetta. b.

1966
nil.

1967
Macushla of Hollesley. b.

1968
Balthazar of Kisumu. d.
Threebees Friar of Copenore. d.
Taddington Diamond Lil of Farnaby.
Tuppence of Blackroc.

1969
nil.

1970
Bardolph of Copenore. d.
Cornhaye Whitsun Bee. b.
Petalouda of Hollesley. b.

1971
Baron Spencer of Buckhall. d.
Cornhaye Kennet. d.
Gelert of Pynesfarm. d.
Jasper of Kisumu. d.

1972
Cleopatra of Hollesley. b.
Copenore Mary Ellen. b.
Meps Portia. b.

1973
Canonbury Eminance of Gildasan. d.
Hollesley Macushlas Dagda.
Hollesley Macushlas Sheba.

1974
Copenore Rab.
Overnoons Mr Micawber of Buckhall.
d.
Celerity Copenore Petronella. b.

1975
Canonbury Autobiography. d.
Lord Jim of Buckhall. d.
Copenore Czarina. b.
Meps Nydia. b.

1976
Master Sirius of Buckhall. d.
Presidents Lad of Bulliff. d.
Artifax Arabella of Farnaby. b.
Astelle Oven Ready of Bulliff. b.

1977
Caemes King Edward of Jilgrajon. d.
Devil Dancer of Hollesley. b.
Jakote Lady Glencora. b.
Jilgragon Lady Victoria. b.

1978
Forefoot Prince of Darkness. d.
The Devil from Wayside. d.
The Devils Advocate of Hollesley. d.
Daredevil of Hollesley. d.
Farnaby Rainy Patch. b.
Forefoot Little Emily of Bredwardine.
b.
Saraband of Eddington. b.

1979
Forefoot Prince Igor of Bredwardine.
d.
Craigavon Emma. b.

1980
Grangemoor Bevis. d.
Langton of Falmore. d.
Hollesley Medicine Man. d.
Countess Carolina. b.
Yarme Susan of Farnaby. b.
Honeycroft Cristmas Cracker. b.
Silver Ghost of Gildasan. b.

1981
Jilgrajon Sir Gladstone. d.
Yarme Jane of Farnaby. b.
Hollesley Rowella. b.

1982
Parcwood W. Bear Esq. of Lesdon. d.
Honeycroft Danny Boy. d.
Smudge of Cornhaye. b.
Darkling Bridie. b.
Jilgrajon Rebecca West. b.
Misty Moondrops of Glynpedr. b.

1983
Forefoot King Kong. d.
Longendalee King Louis. d.
Balclutha Minerva. b.
Bulliff Petrina of Devarro. b.

1984
Bellabees Blunder of Bredwardine. d.
Captain Morgan of Glynpedr. d.
Lord Bernard of Longendale. d.
Bellabees Cader Idris. b.
Bredwardine Beau Ide'al. b.
Craigavon Selina. b.

1985
Darkling Casper. d.
Celerity Powerful Sort. d.
Faerdorn Big Daddy. d.
Luckhurst Goliath. d.
Zanfi Princess Tanya of Damaria. b.
Glynpedr Taittinger. b.

1986
Bulliff Warrior. d.
Trevabyn Black Ice. d.
Hollesley Lord Rupert. d.
Honeycroft Dolly Daydream. b.

Pedigree

OF

Ch: Crown Prince 1051

BREED ..Mastiff..
SEX ..Dog..
COLOUR and MARKINGS ..Fawn..
KENNEL NAME ....
BRED BY ....
OWNED BY ....

Kennel Club Registration Certificate No. ......
Date of Registration ....
Date of Birth ..1880..
Kennel Club Stud Book No. ....
Signed .... Date ......

PARENTS	GRAND-PARENTS	G.G.-PARENTS	G.G.G.-PARENTS	G.G.G.G.-PARENTS	G.G.G.G.G.-PARENTS
SIRE	SIRE Prince	SIRE Rajah 2333	SIRE Griffin	SIRE Prince 2326	Governor 2294
					Duchess 2365
				DAM Nell	Rufus
					Nell
			DAM Phillis 2394	SIRE Wolf 2353	Tiger 2345 (owned by Bill George)
					Why Not
				DAM Phoebe	Governor 2294
					Duchess 2365
		DAM Queen 2396	SIRE Druid 2290	SIRE Wallace	Bruce 2
					Bounty
				DAM Juno	
			DAM Phillis 2394	SIRE Wolf 2353	Tiger 2345
					Why Not
				DAM Phoebe	Governor 2294
					Duchess
	DAM Venus	SIRE Monarch	SIRE	SIRE	
			DAM	DAM	
Young Prince		DAM Juno	SIRE Griffin	SIRE Prince 2326	Governor 2294
					Duchess
				DAM Nell	Rufus
					Nell
			DAM Phillis 2394	SIRE Wolf 2353	Tiger 2345
					Why Not
				DAM Phoebe	Governor 2294
					Duchess 2365

PARENTS	GRAND-PARENTS	G.G.-PARENTS	G.G.G.-PARENTS	G.G.G.G.-PARENTS	G.G.G.G.G.-PARENTS
DAM	**SIRE** The Shah 4457	**SIRE** Rajah 2333	**SIRE** Griffin	**SIRE** Prince 2326	Governor 2294 / Duchess 2365
				DAM Nell	Rufus / Nell
			DAM Phillis	**SIRE** Wolf 2353	Tiger 2345 / Why Not
				DAM Phoebe	Governor 2294 / Duchess 2365
		DAM Ino	**SIRE** Barron 2282	**SIRE** King 2301	Rufus / Nell
				DAM Treasure	Governor 2294 / Venus
			DAM Nell	**SIRE** Turk 2349	King / Hilda
				DAM Duchess	Leo / Venus
Merlin 10585	**SIRE** Rhoda 5338	**SIRE** Rupert	**SIRE** Lion	**SIRE** Rufus (owned by Lukey)	Governor 2294 / Jenny
				DAM Nell	Quaker 2330 / Nell
			DAM Brenda 2359	**SIRE** Quaker (Nichols)	
				DAM Venus (Nichols)	
		DAM Venus	**SIRE** Turk 2349	**SIRE** King 2301	Rufus / Nell
				DAM Hilda	Quaker / Venus
			DAM Countess	**SIRE** No recorded pedigree	
				DAM	

Pedigree
OF
Ch: Bill of Havengore

BREED ..Mastiff.....................

SEX ..Dog.............................

COLOUR and MARKINGS ....

KENNEL NAME.......................

BRED BY ..Mrs. L. Scheerboom.....................

OWNED BY ...Mrs. L. Scheerboom.....................

Kennel Club Registration Certificate No. ......

Date of Registration.....................

Date of Birth ....

Kennel Club Stud Book No........................

Signed .... Date..........

PARENTS	GRAND-PARENTS	G.G.-PARENTS	G.G.G.-PARENTS
SIRE Master Beowulf	**SIRE** Beowulf	**SIRE** Survivor	**SIRE** Adam
			DAM Oscott Norah
		DAM Berenice	**SIRE** Ch: Ronald Widmere
			DAM Buena Ventura
	DAM Jessica	**SIRE** King of the North	**SIRE** Survivor
			DAM Girlie (unregistered)
		DAM Marwood Pride	**SIRE** Stapleford Pedro (unregistered)
			DAM Connie (unregistered probably cross bred)
DAM Crescent Rowena	**SIRE** Duke of Ashenhurst	**SIRE** Adamite	**SIRE** Count Willington
			DAM Adams Last
		DAM Tilly Dunn	**SIRE** Thunderbolt
			DAM Jessie Marton
	DAM Shirebrook Lady (Bullmastiff cross)	**SIRE** Ch: King Baldur	**SIRE** Ch: John Bull
			DAM Ch: Young Mary Bull
		DAM Penkhull Lady (Bullmastiff cross)	**SIRE** Stapleford Agrippa (Bullmastiff)
			DAM Helen (unregistered)

Pedigree of first Mastiff litter bred by Mrs. Scheerboom. 10 May 1925.

Registered as a Mastiff

BREED..(details unknown)..................
SEX...Dog.........................
COLOUR and MARKINGS....................
KENNEL NAME.........................
BRED BY..........................
OWNED BY.........................

Pedigree

OF

Probable Pedigree of Templecombe Taurus

(see text)

....

Kennel Club Registration Certificate No. .....
Date of Registration.................
Date of Birth.....................
Kennel Club Stud Book No.................
Signed........................ Date......

PARENTS	GRAND-PARENTS	G.G.-PARENTS	G.G.G.-PARENTS	G.G.G.G.-PARENTS
SIRE	**SIRE**	**SIRE** Ch. Simba	**SIRE** Ch: Athos	Farcroft Fidelity
				Noble
Burngreave Baron (Fawn bullmastiff)	Millbrook Bruce		**DAM** Lady Athena	Ch. Tiger Prince
				Pridzors Princess
		DAM Barneshill Betty	**SIRE** Ch: Tiger Prince	Tiger Torus
				Princess Poppy
			DAM Pridzors Princess	Tiger Torus
				Pridzors Belle
	DAM	**SIRE** Tenzson	**SIRE** Ch: Tenz	Vindictive Prince
				Princess Ursula
	Lady Chita		**DAM** Donna Clara	Don Juan
				Millicent of Westview
		DAM Poppy	**SIRE** Ch: Roger of the Fenns	Don Juan
				Luzlow Princess
			DAM Bagnall Queen	Tiger Torus
				Tiger Princess
DAM	**SIRE**	**SIRE** Paladin of Deleval	**SIRE** Goldhawk Imperator	Ch: Cedric of Ashenhurst
				Goldhawk Fairy
Chenda (Brindle mastiff)	Bayard of Deleval		**DAM** Torfreda of Deleval	Ch: Bil of Mavengore
				Gyda of Deleval
		DAM Glorianna of Deleval	**SIRE** Sioux Chief	Ch: Cleveland Premier
				Goldhawk Jasmine
			DAM Tess of Brookwood	Ch: Duke
				Bess of Brongarth
	DAM	**SIRE** Hereward of Deleval	**SIRE** Rey of Oakwood	Ch: Cedric of Ashenhurst
				Brunhilda
	Gundreda of Deleval		**DAM** Naida of Deleval	Ch: Bill of Havengore
				Gyda of Deleval
		DAM Joanna of Deleval	**SIRE** Cleveland Comedian	Ch: Woden
				Lady Demisa of Harding
			DAM Cleveland Joy	Robert of Hellingly
				Fair Freda of Wantley

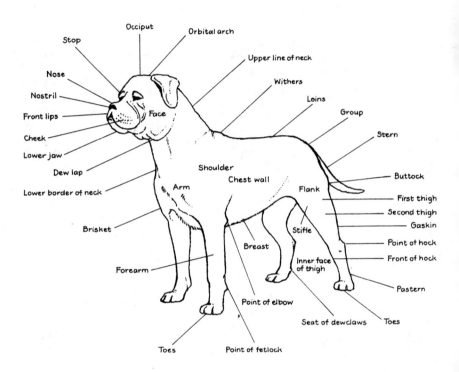

Occiput

Orbital arch

Stop

Upper line of neck

Nose

Withers

Nostril

Loins

Front lips

Group

Face

Cheek

Stern

Lower jaw

Dew lap

Shoulder

Lower border of neck

Buttock

Arm

Chest wall

Flank

First thigh

Brisket

Second thigh

Gaskin

Stifle

Point of hock

Breast

Front of hock

Forearm

Inner face
of thigh

Pastern

Point of elbow

Toes

Seat of dewclaws

Toes

Point of fetlock

Points of a Molosser

List of Bullmastiff Champions

(The date is that of the Kennel Club Stud Book recording champion status)

1960
Alard of Buttonoak. d.
Marcus of Boardy. d.
Bambino. b.
Bulstaff Prudence of Torthorwald. b.

1961
Ambrose of Edialhouse. d.
Mi Brandy of Marbette. d.
Buttonoak Appeal of Gimingham. b.
Joyeuse of Goodstock. b.
Joyful Lass of Goodstock. b.
Mi Hope of Marbette. b.
Sweetie of Pillard. b.

1962
Fronshane Strang. d.
Master Brandy of Marbette. d.
Oldwell Mi Trooper of Marbette. d.
Romper Lad of Goodstock. d.

1963
Bulstaff Achilles. d.
Bulstaff Brobdingnag. d.
Burghley of Bullturn. d.
Goodstock Bash On. d.
Dancer of Oldwell. b.
Bulstaff Leah. b.

1964
Buttonoak Meg of Marbette. b.
Duchess of Oldwell. b.
Goodstock Twinkletoes. b.
Lucinda of Cheyenne. b.

21965
Dandini Prince of Oldwell. d.
Hakmaluk of Naukeen. b.
Morejoy Pride Amanda. b.

1966
Goodstock Gay Kavalier. d.
Jupiter of Sandene. d.
Oldwell Toby of Studberg. d.
Miss Oldwell. b.
Regina of Ivywill. b.

1967
Yorkist Minstrel. d.
Goodstock Don Juan. d.
Shabaka of Sandene. d.
Taurus of Mureken. d.
Trina of Ty Fynnon. b.
Triumph Herald of Mureken. b.

1968
Darrell of Kelwall. d.
Harvester of Lombardy. d.
Wyaston Tudor Prince. d.
Yorkist Magician of Oldwell. d.
Gimingham Royal Flush. b.
Morejoy Eastern Princess. b.

1969
Mister of Oldwell. d.
Regent of Oldwell. d.
Derry of Kelwall. d.
Little Miss of Oldwell. b.
Myrtle of Oldwell. b.

1970
Showell Zarbor. d.
Bulstaff Rosalynde. b.
Bulstaff Topsy. b.
Oldwell Queen Gwenivive of
    Mureken. b.

1971
Bulstaff Revelry. d.
Claude of Oldwell. d.
Rommel of Ivywill. d.
Kwintra Tammy of Ty Fynnon. b.
Yorkist Maid Marion. b.
Pekingtown Abece. b.

1972
Pitmans Gentleman Jim. d.
Copperfield Martin Chuzzlewit. d.

1973
Lombardy Simon of Silverfarm. d.
Pitmans Sir Albert. d.
Stephan of Naukeen. d.
Thorfin of Oldwell. d.
Copperfield Sarah Pocket. b.

1974
Lombardy Tristram. d.
Showell Yibor. d.
Hannah of Oldwell. b.
Naukeen Loraine. b.

1975
Bunsoro Cloudburst. d.
Frederick of Kelwall. d.
Doomwatch Gipsy of Oldwell. b.
Bulstaff Heritage of Ellney. b.
Yorkist Miss Muffet. b.

1976
Yorkist Marquis. d.
Copperfield Ben Allen. d.
Nicholas of Oldwell. d.
Leyrigg Rhinestone Ruby. b.

1977
Bulstaff Solomon. d.
Craigylea Sir Galahad. d.
Doomwatch Brigand. d.
Erazmus of Oldwell. d.
Bunsoro Donna. b.
Bonnie of Kelwall. b.
Colom Florin. b.
Simbec Clarissa of Oldwell. b.

1978
Copperfield Sam Weller. d.
Bunsoro Dianna. b.
Bunsoro Penny Lane. b.
Honey Bee of Oldwell. b.

1979
Naukeen Ranger. d.
Blaze of Oldwell. d.
Frazer of Oldwell. d.
Milbarsa Man Friday of Lystan. d.
Pitmans Buccaneer. d.
Naukeen Leila. b.
Verona of Oldwell. b.

1980
Clyde of Kelwall. d.
Kracka of Oldwell. d.
Lombardy Llewellyn. d.
Maggie May of Bunsoro. b.
Copperfield Maria Lobbs. b.
Crystal of Oldwell. b.
Doomwatch Juanita of Oldwell. b.

1981
Leyrigg Tora-Tora. d.
Purston Harvest Gold. d.
Bombadillo of Bunsoro. d.
Bunsoro Bombadier. d.
Todomas Duchess. b.

1982
Bunsoro Buzcock. d.
Colom Jumbo. d.
Pitmans Deputy. d.
Todomas Tanya of Bunsoro. b.
Bryany Rima Renown. b.
Bunsoro Proud Mary. b.
Colom Nelly. b.
Daffreda of Kelwall. b.
Star of Oldwell. b.
Todomas Tamar. b.

1983
Mystro of Oldwell. d.
Twynfields Bryden. d.
Leyrigg Maurven Sweet Water. b.
Coombelane River Worle. b.

1984
Barnaby of Oldwell. d.
Carndearg El Toro De Oro. d.
Leyrigg Major Callum. d.
Lombardy Harvey. d.
Seafoam Miranda. b.
Tartruffe Arachne. b.
Ivywill Wagga Wagga of Colom. b.
Justmaro Esta. b.

1985
Naukeen Major Kew of Eastlynn. d.
Barrus Beaumont. d.
Copperfield Pip. d.
Graecia Centaur. d.
Jagopeeko Inam of Oldwell. d.
Naukeen Daniel. d.
Jagopeeko Inara. b.
Linzie of Oldwell. b.
Naukeen Melody of Dreadnot. b.
Todomas Tanya of Bunsoro. b.

1986
Coldstream of Bunsoro. d.
Sharwells Mean Mr Mustard of
  Pitmans. d.
Tartruffe Apollo. d.
Wyburn Rula of Oldwell. d.
Wyburn Tarna. b.
Jostmaro Mascorade of Oldwell. b.
Sapphire of Oldwell. d.
Sylva of Oldwell. b.
Zeela of Oldwell. b.

Pedigree

OF

Ch: Roger of the Fens

BREED .. Bull Mastiff
SEX .. Dog.
COLOUR and MARKINGS .. Fawn.
KENNEL NAME ......
BRED BY .. G. J. Wedgewood.
OWNED BY ......

Kennel Club Registration Certificate No. ......
Date of Registration ......
Date of Birth .. Nov. 1929.
Kennel Club Stud Book No. ......
Signed ...... Date ......

PARENTS	GRAND-PARENTS	G.G.-PARENTS	G.G.G.-PARENTS	G.G.G.G.-PARENTS	G.G.G.G.G.-PARENTS
SIRE	**SIRE** Farcroft Fascist	**SIRE** Farcroft Fidelity	**SIRE** Shireland Vindictive	**SIRE** Vindictive	Wellington Marquis (Bulldog)
					Nuneaton Nance
				DAM Bulwell Vixen	
			DAM Farcroft Faithful	**SIRE** Bullwell Cezar	
				DAM Hamil Vixen	Crossbred Mastiff/Bulldog
		DAM Farcroft Crystal	**SIRE** Farcroft Pedro	**SIRE** Thorneywood Terror	
				DAM Broomspring Vixen	
			DAM Farcroft Agate	**SIRE** Osmaston Viper	
				DAM Almscliffe Betty	
Don Juan	**DAM** Pride of Birches Head	**SIRE** Baldurs Best	**SIRE** Ch: King Baldur Mastiff, born 8.6.1917	**SIRE** Ch: Young John Bull (Mastiff)	
				DAM Ch: Young Mary Bull (Mastiff)	(Crossbred Bulldog/Mastiff)
			DAM Penkhull Lady	**SIRE** Stapleford Agrippa	
				DAM Helen (Mastiff)	
		DAM Athena	**SIRE** Farcroft Fidelity	**SIRE** Shireland Vindictive	
				DAM Farcroft Faithfull	
			DAM Wulston Molly	**SIRE** Demon Max	Unrecorded pedigree—probably crossbred
				DAM Ven 2	

216

PARENTS	GRAND-PARENTS	G.G.-PARENTS	G.G.G.-PARENTS	G.G.G.G.-PARENTS	G.G.G.G.G.-PARENTS
DAM Luzlow Princess	**SIRE** Ch: Tiger Prince	**SIRE** Tiger Torus	**SIRE** Farcroft Fidelity	**SIRE** Shireland Vindictive	
				DAM Farcroft Faithful	
			DAM Farcroft Storm	**SIRE** Farcroft Dauntless	
				DAM Farcroft Defence	
		DAM Princess Poppy	**SIRE** Brutus of Park Vale	**SIRE** Bulwell Muggins	
				DAM Bess	
			DAM Borrace of Dartmoor	**SIRE** Woolley	
				DAM Panther	
	DAM Pridzors Princess	**SIRE** Tiger Torus	**SIRE** Farcroft Fidelity	**SIRE** Shireland Vindictive	
				DAM Farcroft Faithful	
			DAM Farcroft Storm	**SIRE** Farcroft Dauntless	
				DAM Farcroft Defence	
		DAM Pridzors Belle	**SIRE** Tiger Torus	**SIRE** Farcroft Fidelity	
				DAM Farcroft Storm	
			DAM Bertha (Mastiff)	**SIRE** Unregistered Mastiffs	
				DAM Unregistered Mastiffs	

Pedigree of Ch: King See page 31

```
                                                   Garnier's Lion
                                 Lukey's Governor
                                                   Lukey's Countess
                 Lukey's Rufus
                                 Horn's Jenny ———— parentage unknown

Ch:
King
                                                   Thompson's Saladin
                                 Cauntley's Quaker
                                                   Thompson's Duchess
                 Field's Nell 3
                                                   unknown sire
                                 Nell 2
                                                   Lord Darnley's Nell ———— Parentage unknown but Wynn
                                                                            considered her to be from a
                                                                            Bull Mastiff dog and mastiff bitch
```